SYMPHONY
of the SOUL

8 Tools for Finding Joy After Loss

CLAUDIA C. CASTILLO

ISBN: 979-8-9896395-0-2 - paperback
ISBN: 979-8-9896395-1-9 - ebook
ISBN: 979-8-9896395-2-6 - hardcover

TABLE OF CONTENTS

I dedicate this book to parents and families suffering from the effects of addiction.

Access for free our exclusive video to heal your heart.

Discover 8 simple exercises that I practice daily with my loved ones, empowering me to open and connect with my spine. I sincerely hope they contribute to your journey as well.

Join our mindful community and participate in future events!

chateodelcorazon.com/giftvideo

FOREWORD

Modern life is characterized by hustle, bustle, and dissatisfaction.

Even though our advanced technological developments have immense advantages, they have not helped us to find fulfillment as individuals or connect us all at higher levels of consciousness.

More than two thirds of the world's population have a smart phone or computer and yet we find ourselves divided and further apart each day. Levels of loneliness, depression, and lack of communication keep rising.

Our children and youth are crushed by the pressures of social media and its demands for "likes" and acceptance. The violence, bullying, attacks, indiscriminate mockery, and even lynching through social networks corner our young ones into anesthetizing themselves from the pain of living, among other things through the use of chemicals, tobacco, food, or codependency.

Sharing her vulnerability, honesty, and luminous spirit, Claudia C. Castillo invites us to join her, in Symphony of the Soul, on an uncompromising journey into the depths of her heart to learn how addiction managed to take Álvaro Luis, her young son, away from this plane.

Álvaro Luis' intense relationships with his parents, siblings, and friends, has given them signals to help them rediscover the world, reconnect with themselves, and surrender themselves unreservedly to a life full of possibilities.

Sharing her journey of transformation is not only Claudia C. Castillo's tribute to her son but also a hopeful example for readers who have not been able to free themselves from the constraints and prejudices that limit their days and obstruct their relationships with others.

Claudia C. Castillo urges us to wake up and play the best notes in our soul for the world and everyone around us to hear.

Lolita Ayala
Dolores "Lolita" Ayala Nieto is a Mexican journalist and philanthropist
Mexico City, Spring 2023

INTRODUCTION

Álvaro Luis was twenty-six years old and had his whole life ahead of him when he died from a heroin[1] overdose. He was one of the thousands of victims the opioid epidemic claimed. He had such a unique artistic sensibility and a great passion for travel, architecture, photography, music and people. He was my son.

The same day we went to touch his cold body, to recognize him, he had been expelled from the rehabilitation center because he was caught with a beer in his hand. He got it for free at the club. He had no money, they were not allowed to have any at the center, but he escaped to the club in an Uber, and they gave it to him there for free.

That morning he called his brother to tell him what had happened and said, "Don't worry, I'm go-

---

1 Fetanyl is an opioid that is said to be 50 times stronger than heroin and about 100 times stronger than morphine. It is severely impacting American youth, leading to a rise in drug overdoses and fatalities. Its potency, availability on the black market, and low cost make it attractive to young individuals who may be unaware of its lethal nature.

ing to apologize and convince them to let me in again, there won't be a problem."

When we were notified of his expulsion from the center, I immediately thought about going to pick him up, I wanted to save him, as usual, but I talked to another one of my sons and to their uncle, an expert in recovery, and they both told me to "let go and let God." The phrase that I had been taught and made to repeat thousands of times at the Twelve Steps. I didn't go get him, but I did go visit another recovery center where the director said to me, "Ma'am, I know you want your child to heal, but he is the one who has to want to recover."

I've had to understand that my son was not truly mine, he never was. Healing his addiction was only up to him; I couldn't do it, but I tried anyway. I tried absolutely everything! I did the best I could with the level of consciousness that I had at the time.

The most difficult thing about my grieving process, of all that I had to go through in order to restore myself, to grow, raise my level of consciousness, and accept that Álvaro had left his physical body and was no longer in this world, has been to forgive myself (and I will talk about forgiveness in the first chapter)—forgiving myself for having thought that

I had the power and control to save my son. Forgiving myself for my lack of humility when I think that if I had picked him up at the program where he was, if I had taken him to another program, if I had canceled his Uber service, or had left him without cell phone coverage, if I had done something—or everything—different, I could have saved him. Forgiving myself for thinking that I could have caused his illness, that I was able to control or cure the disease of addiction.

It is inevitable to look back and wonder if, for example, not having sent him to Canada would have been better. At that time, however, during his high school years, we were convinced that spending some time away from Miami's atmosphere, which was terrible at the moment, would do him good. We wanted him to spend some time away from that extremely athletic and competitive society that he had such a hard time integrating into, because, although he liked sports, he did not see well, and between that, his ADHD and his learning deficiencies, belonging had been difficult for him ever since he was a kid.

From the start, he had problems with his eyesight (amblyopia, or lazy eye), which was corrected a little over the years, but as a child, he had been recommended to wear googles, or protective glasses to make sure his one good eye wasn't accidentally hurt. I remember how cute he looked with his red glasses; he was beautiful. He had a very good athletic disposition. He was not fast, but he was strong and enthusiastic and he loved sports. Álvaro's problem was seeing and following the ball with his eyes. When at age five, he played baseball, even the moms commented, "What's wrong with him? Why doesn't he hit the ball?" And since the culture around him placed emphasis on athletics and academics, he did not have as much of an opportunity to develop his strengths, his artistic gifts, which were the ones in which he stood out the most: he was an artist.

On his psychological evaluation he wrote:

"It would be better if school didn't exist!"

"The biggest problem in my life is homework!"

The truth is that Álvaro Luis suffered in school.

We provided all the support we could and enrolled him in all kinds of academic courses, as well as extracurricular artistic and sports activities that we thought would help him. We wanted him to feel *cool*, like everyone else. He got his black belt in karate and became a member of the tennis team. Here I must confess that—although thanks to his wonderful coach Daniel, Álvaro played great tennis—it was due to my insistence that he made the team. "Listen, coach, my son is very good. He just entered a new school, I think he needs this to connect, I really think he needs it," and I asked, almost begged him, to accept Álvaro.

Looking back, I understand that at that point it was no longer my role to talk to the coach, to want to control my son's integration into the high school tennis team, but I wanted to help him because I realized that he was suffering. That was proof of my codependency, my addiction. We are all addicted, as we will discover in the next chapters. Not only are there drug and alcohol addictions, but we also have many other addictive behaviors that we must identify.

"I will make this child succeed!" It's an obsession we have, this need to live the lives of others. We don't realize it's a kind of disease: your child must live his life and you must live yours. You think, as a mother, as a father, that your children are your art, your project.

While at school in Canada, he developed a codependent relationship with his computer and the limitless world that he discovered through it. He spent hours watching movies instead of studying or even sleeping, and since the computer was a study tool through which they took their exams and studied, there was no one really monitoring either the time they spent on it or the content they accessed. It became his escape. He felt connected to everything out there, but really, he became disconnected from everything and everyone, especially himself. That was the worst. On one occasion, when I went to visit him, a teacher said to me, "If he were my son, I wouldn't leave him here."

We brought him back to Miami so he could continue his high school education there. I saw and felt strange things, I had my suspicions that he consumed something, but my husband insisted that his attitude was normal, part of the age, that he was not consuming anything. I remember that I found it strange, for example, that when his wisdom teeth were removed, he insisted so much on keeping the pain medication that the dentist prescribed, in his room. He said he wanted to take it alone, without me monitoring or being on top of him.

A former police officer that we hired had him take a polygraph test and what the exam showed was that, although it was true that he did not use recreational drugs, he was using excessive: amphetamines and painkillers. As is very well known, especially after the opioid epidemic, these substances are tremendously addictive and very easy to obtain. At first, he took them to relieve his emotional pain, but then they became indispensable for him to live. Until they took his life.

Once he graduated from high school, it was time to go to college. The truth is that Álvaro should not have gone, and I sensed it, but I was surrounded by people immersed in the process of applications and I was sucked into that obsession of helping my son go to college, and a good one. I felt that he wasn't ready to go, but everyone told me that they get grounded there, that it's part of the experience. The lady who helped us with his applications and the whole process said to me, "They will mature." Or not, as in the case of Álvaro.

He went to a Jesuit college, Xavier, in Cincinnati, OH, because my husband has a Jesuit spirit and is very religious. It's a great university. I visited it and sensed that the atmosphere was beautiful. I felt that perhaps it would help him take a turn. He learned guitar, languages, and chose many artistic subjects. Then he did a summer here in Miami, at

UM, and I saw him better than ever. But then he went back to Cincinnati and stubbornly insisted to live in a basement by himself, and that was a disaster. What he wanted, in addition, was to go to New York. He had become obsessed with the city since he visited it at age seventeen, so he made the move there, to The New School, a private progressive university for intellectuals and artists. He was there for two or three years until his aunts from NY called us one day to tell us that he had arrived to visit them with a bag that had needles. We realized then (and it was confirmed to us by a specialist my husband consulted) that he was using heroin.

In my desperation, I looked for a shaman, and we sent Álvaro with him to the mountains of Utah for two or three months. It seemed like everything was going well, but then that same shaman convinced us that Álvaro was ready to go back to NY. So, he returned to NY, alongside the shaman . . . and he got lost again. The shaman thought he could control him, but he escaped and started consuming once more. One of the main characteristics of heroin is that it is unnoticeable, until it is too late.

He then came to Miami to seek healing. We took him to addiction experts and tried everything, from the use of Ibogaine, a natural psychoactive substance that Álvaro tried twice outside the United States because it was (and still is) banned here, to opioid replacement therapy with Methadone and Suboxone, which was the recommended and legal treatment.

One day talking to Álvaro, he told me: "Well, Mom, if it had been smoking, you would have been able to smell it; alcohol you would have been able to smell, too. But not the painkillers." However, long before that talk, when during his high school years, I sensed he had a problem with alcohol or drugs, and everyone told me that I was imagining things. My biggest fear was that he would end up in jail. "If they put him in jail, what do I do?" So, I found an online course to support prisoners, *Mindfulness for Prisoners*, taught by Fleet Maull, founder and CEO of Heart Mind Institute. I became certified and started volunteering in prisons.

I think my soul unconsciously knew that prison was not my greatest fear, though. Deep down inside, my most terrifying fear, although it was not possible for me to recognize it at a conscious level, was that of losing my son, and it attracted what seemed like synchronicities. One day getting a manicure, for example, the woman next to me turned out to be the director of the Children's Bereavement Center, a support program for people who have lost loved ones, that Ransom Everglades School in Miami supported by lending its space on Monday nights. I volunteered there, too. I was commissioned to a group of small children. We would give them magazines so they could find and cut out things that reminded them of their parents. I remember a five-year-old boy who cut out about fifty tennis shoes. His dad had been killed in Venezuela while having his bicycle stolen, and for some reason the sneakers reminded him of his dad.

I'm glad to have participated in that program a few years before losing my son because the experience helped me observe all the different ways in which human beings face death. One felt directly connected with death there.

In that space, I clearly understood that very well-known quote from philosopher Epictetus that states, "It's not what happens to you, but how you react to it that matters." I personally feel—today, after much inner work—that we should not fear death because the truth is that death connects us with a new dimension, a dimension in which you know and feel that the person who left before us is in. From there, they love and protect us without ceasing to exist; they remain with us in a spiritual way. My son's spiritual strength has totally changed me and helps me every day to make better decisions and turn my pain into wisdom so that I can help and support others.

I spent two years volunteering in prisons, two in the Children's Bereavement Center, and I also took the Landmark course for the development of consciousness. In addition, I worked with a Mount Sinai psychiatrist who needed a life coach to supplement his patients with tapping, hugs and all sorts of energy tools. For me that work was healing because, even though I could not help my son, I could help those young men.

Fleet Maull had another course, a ten-day silent retreat that I signed up for, but ended up going to once my son had died: ten whole days of breathing and crying.

My son Álvaro Luis, too, was enrolled to go to a retreat, a yoga retreat with Tommy Rosen, addiction recovery expert; however, he died a few days before and could not make it. We decided then to attend as a family, the four of us: his parents and his two brothers. We went to celebrate his life and to participate in the yoga retreat for recovery during which we felt that Álvaro's love and presence manifested itself in many undisputable ways. That experience strengthened us as a family. And there, Tommy, the director of the course, told me (and always repeats this to me), "Nothing you could have done would have changed Álvaro's life. Don't torture yourself with made-up stories."

I did the best I could.

Tommy Rosen founded and directs Recovery 2.0, a program that not only helps you recover from addiction, but also improves your life exponentially. I understood immediately that this was, without a doubt, the most complete program, the one with the most potential. But it was in its developing stages at that time, so in some way, my family and I became founding members of that movement that today is preeminent and huge.

Álvaro took pictures of everything. It was almost an exaggeration. We would be driving in the middle of the I-95 highway in front of Wynwood, and he would exclaim, "Stop, Mommy! Stop here!" because he wanted that photo. He had a magical eye; he would take the pictures and then edit them.

When he died and I felt all that emptiness, I would spend hours looking at his photos, and every day of insomnia, when I woke up at four in the morning and it was impossible to go back to sleep, I got a different message. I would look at a particular photograph and think a message; it came to me. I felt then that his art was letting me know what I needed in order to heal and to share with the world to help others heal.

One day when I was awake but hadn't gotten up to write at 4 a.m., a paper mâché figurine that Álvaro Luis made when he was only twelve years old dropped from my cabinet with a thump. I think the message couldn't have been clearer: "Get up and keep writing."

This book integrates all the messages that my son transmitted to me, both in life and after his death, messages that help to manage stress, to restore you, to raise the level of consciousness. I learned that to recover from any situation you are experiencing, it is necessary to consider mind, body, emotions and spirit: all our aspects in their totality.

Each chapter begins with a sample of Álvaro's art, one of his mosaics, as well as the message that came to me while I was looking at it during a particular morning.

Thanks to my son, I learned that the society in which we operate today is addicted to many things, such as food, technology and people, among others, and this has been normalized, unfortunately, and affects our relationships, values, meaning and purpose of life. Thanks to him, I discovered a much deeper connection with my inner self and developed great compassion for all of us who suffer from addictions. I thank him for having brought so much love into our lives, and I am grateful for the pain I experienced with his death, because thanks to that, I can feel that we belong to each other, that we are all interconnected. Thanks to the liberation of my son, I have raised my level of consciousness and I have learned to live happier and with greater peace. Today it is clear to me that you do not choose to be an addict, but the responsibility to recover is one hundred percent your own.

The purpose of this book is to honor Álvaro and help others heal. My desire is that you find in it a word, an idea, a message, or a tool that can help you transform your life and support you to achieve the best version of yourself. In the following chapters, I will explain the tools and techniques with which

I have been able to embrace and love my pain, and mostly, to heal.

You can read it from beginning to end or open it at any random page or chapter and explore the support and healing techniques that can help you, from getting through the day, if you're having a very difficult one, to increasing your level of consciousness.

I thank Álvaro Luis for guiding me to write it, and you for reading it.

"Perhaps the healing of the world rests on just this sort of shift in our way of seeing, a coming to know that in our suffering and in our joy, we are connected to one another with unbreakable and compelling human bonds."
Rachel Naomi Remen

CHAPTER 1

Forgiveness

The only way to understand and process everything is by forgiving. Your presence is infinite: your spirit is my spirit; your peace is my peace.

Grand Canyon, Colorado

My son Álvaro no longer inhabits this earthly realm, but his presence is infinite. When I am attentive and connected, his powerful spirit reveals itself in different forms. I know that my son exists in another dimension because I feel him, like when I'm crying or I'm sad and a rainbow appears, I know then that he is there. In the movement of flowers, in the singing of birds, in the depth of a canyon; I find his presence above all in nature.

My son's spirit manifests itself in many ways. I will share one of these divine manifestations with you.

Three days before the fourth anniversary of his death, on a Saturday, we went to a concert by the prodigious Gabriela Montero, my father's favorite pianist. For her encore, she asked the audience to hum the melody of what they'd like, and most of the audience hummed "Alma llanera." We all really enjoyed the Venezuelan piece and Gabriela Montero's incredible talent.

The next day, Sunday morning, I attended a presentation of several books, and one of the authors delighted us by singing a song that turned out to be, again, "Alma llanera." "Well, what a coincidence," I thought, and out of curiosity I looked up the definition of the word *llanera*, which means "healthy and robust."

On Monday, the day of his anniversary, I was in the office with a very young girl, Sofia, who was helping me with computer issues when suddenly, she said, "My great-grandfather wrote the song 'Alma llanera.'" Now I really laugh, and I thank God for the beautiful message that my son Álvaro Luis has sent me: his soul is healthy and robust. This is the way in which my son shows up in my life.

I am immensely grateful for my son's spiritual manifestations and confirm daily that his presence is infinite. The only thing I must do is be aware and present to feel it. My son Álvaro is my hero; he is my protector and has strength for two; his secret weapon is love.

Forgiving myself has been the biggest challenge I have faced during my grieving and restorative process. I forgive myself and then I forgive myself again, every day. I forgive myself, as I mentioned in the introduction, for thinking that I was in control of saving my son. I forgive myself for the lack of humility I show when I think that maybe if I had gone to pick him up at the center where he was, if I had taken him to another program, if I had canceled his Uber service, if I had left him without cell service, if I had done something—or everything—different, I could have saved him. I forgive myself because my ego deceives me by making me believe that I can exert control over a superior plan, that of the Universe, regarding life. I forgive myself for believing that I was capable of healing him, of fixing it all. I forgive myself for thinking that I could have caused his illness, that I had the power to control or cure addiction.

During my healing process, it has been crucial to forgive myself for my behavior and for any words that may have contributed in some way to exacerbate my son's illness. I forgive myself for living in so much fear. I forgive myself for not being able to be an example for Álvaro and help him understand that everything we need is inside us, to understand that there is a pharmacy within ourselves, that our endocrine system is an infinite pharmacy.

I've also had to forgive others for not knowing or understanding the appropriate and truthful way to support a person dealing with the disease of addiction. We all did the best we could with the level of consciousness we had.

Sometimes the hardest thing is to forgive our loved ones, our relatives. In order to forgive our parents or ancestors, it helps to imagine what they suffered. We must consider the traumas that may have been part of their childhood and which they may not have been able to process yet.

Forgive everyone for everything! Forgive everything because only by doing so can we heal and get unstuck in our lives. The Holy Bible tells us to forgive "seventy times seven."

Seventy times seven, because one must forgive over and over again, repetitively, until you achieve real forgiveness.

Forgiveness requires intense work, but when we are finally able to forgive ourselves and others fully, our perception will shift, blame will transform into blessing and hurt into healing: we will be liberated, free, and open to live with peace, love, joy and gratitude.

Time heals wounds, and during that time, deep wounds may help us change our perception of ourselves, help us understand that we can choose how we respond to what happens in our life and choose to do it wisely. Wounds allow light to flow into our lives if we are conscious enough. They help us forgive.

Álvaro's spiritual presence in my life gives me the strength to evolve and become a better version of myself. Ever since my son left to another plane, since he lost his physical body and become a spiritual being, I feel him more present than ever. I feel him in my whole being. I love him immensely, and it is only by thinking about him that my heart rejoices. I forgive him for breaking free from his body before I did. You must forgive the addicted person because his mind has been hijacked.

I choose to forgive myself every day.

Forgiveness does not relieve us, but it does prevent us from suffering twice as much. My contribution to the world's healing, and my own, has been to live with a daily attitude of forgiveness.

> *"To forgive is to release a prisoner*
> *and discover that the prisoner was you."*
> *Lewis B. Smedes*

Heaven's light shines upon us when we abide in love, and it is through forgiveness that we can abide in love.

Today and every day, I decide to forgive and send love to all those who have hurt me consciously or unconsciously, because I know that the greatest test is to love those who are difficult to love.

Forgiveness allows us to keep people in our hearts so that we can heal; it frees us from the chains of past suffering and saves us from repeating whatever traumas may have caused them.

The act of forgiving benefits our health, even if it sometimes takes many years and is a very difficult process.

Radical Forgiveness

I am so grateful to have found an amazing therapy, created by Dr. Colin Tipping, called **Radical Forgiveness**, which I am beginning to practice and want to share with you. It is an extremely powerful process that teaches you to forgive and heal in an easier and faster way. It is based on the premise that everything that happens, happens for a reason; nothing happens by chance. The work is done from the root, and that is why it is called radical.

I briefly list here the five phases on which the process consists, and I invite you to further investigate it if you'd like to learn more about it.

First phase

Telling the story of your pain, your anger, or your indignation; writing it or having it heard by someone and explaining why you are or feel victimized.

Second phase

Feeling the feelings: allowing yourself to feel emotions and feelings by naming them. Emotions are like water because they dissolve and drag everything with them; they connect all the planes of being. Accessing the pain is the beginning of its healing.

Third phase

In this phase, you collapse the story and reduce it to an objective dimension by taking the power out of the victim story, which is mostly interpretation. Facts are separated from interpretations so you can identify what is true. Suffering comes from interpretations because real and objective pain passes, but suffering lingers.

Fourth phase

Honoring the human aspect of the situation, and at the same time being willing to contemplate that there might be a different order, we reframe the story under a spiritual perspective in which everything has a meaning that only the spirit knows. Whether we believe it or not, it does not matter because the transformation of energy takes place anyway, and the layers are unveiled little by little (sometimes it takes time: weeks or months).

Fifth phase

This phase consists of formulating the new perspective and opening oneself to the possibility that this makes sense. Here the transformation is integrated, we root it in our being with some type of physical activity, such as:

- art
- dance
- singing
- breath work

Through these five phases, and thanks to your inner work, something new is created, you reconcile with the story, you release it, transcend it, and achieve forgiveness without anyone knowing (or caring) if you are the victim or victimizer.

Radical forgiveness liberates our soul; it helps us in our spiritual journey; it brings us light and strength to live from the heart; it helps us to raise our consciousness.

During my volunteer service in prison, I understood that the most difficult job prisoners must do to heal and evolve is to forgive themselves and then to be able to forgive loved ones who failed them in their upbringing or were the cause of them growing up with a sense of lack.

It is also necessary to forgive our culture, our society, where excessive consumption of substances is an essential part of everyday life. Our materialistic culture has caused lots of imbalances on the planet. Today while many of us are wearing a COVID-19 mask, I believe the message is that we must consume less of everything and seek silence, learn to listen, and evolve inwardly.

"It is no measure of health to be well adjusted to a profoundly sick society."
Jiddu Krishnamurti

A great example of the spirit of forgiveness is the letter that our son wrote to us with so much love, asking us to forgive him.

Dear Father and Mother,

I do not wish on my worst enemy the problems and pain that a son like me has caused you. The fact that you are still here makes me cry and realize how lucky and blessed I am to have you still in my life. I am committed to living a clean, healthy, happy and productive life.

I want to let you know that for the first time in a long time I am aware. I'm aware of everything and finally understand what that means. I am aware of the hell I have made you go through; I am aware of how much money you have spent on me only to have me relapse again and again. I am aware of all the time I have lost, moving aimlessly through life, trying to see what I can get away with without much effort. And the time I have made you waste trying to help a son who didn't appreciate anything you were doing for him.

I am aware of how I have continued to put my life and yours on hold with my thoughtless actions. I am aware of all the pain, agony, shame and suffering I have caused you. This is why there are no words to express how bad I feel, and I hope that one day you will find in your heart a way to forgive me, once you see how different I am and begin to see how I keep my word and am responsible for myself. I can't find the words to express the gratitude I have for you. When most parents would have given up long ago, you have put up with an unkind child. When I think about everything you have done for me and what I've given you in return, it literally makes my stomach churn. This desire to heal myself has never been stronger. I know what I want to do for the rest of my life, and I know how I should do it, I ask for your help to reach my goals.

Being aware every day makes me feel sad about being where I am at this stage of my life, realizing that I am not where I would have liked to be in my life. Maybe it's the fact that I've finally woken up and fully realize and understand my current situation, I know I might seem too eager to start over, but I feel that this burning energy and desire will really help me fulfill my mission.

I know that I am not in a position to ask you for anything else, especially when you have given me every-thing and I continually lean on you without expressing a drop of gratitude, regret or remorse. The plan is to enroll in the intensive course. To begin to become a creator, to stop living as a helpless victim in action. Being accountable for myself is the most important thing and that starts when I keep my word of completing the real estate licensing course and pass the state exam. Throughout these 10 days I will have to be accountable for myself in the broadest sense of the word. This is what I want to create for myself and the time to start is NOW. I can't keep feeding the wolf of anger and wondering "what if" or "double checking it all", everything is perfect, I need to feed the wolf of love and simply "take it on" and "go for it" "no matter how" and starting with a clean slate and finally letting go of my past. But keeping it as an important teacher who has taught me many valuable lessons.

I love you more than anyone else on this earth and I'm sorry I don't express that every day. Please help me in my search for a new self-sufficient life. I have wasted too much time and prefer to do so with the support of my beloved parents. So, thank you so much for all you have done for me.

Your child who loves you,

Álvaro

Forgiveness is a powerful act of self-love, self-discovery and the unfolding of your true self. It does not erase the memory of an experience or neutralize its impact, but it modifies the interpretation. There is less to forgive when you do not take things personally.

The deepest healing occurs when during the process you find that you can forgive and change what you have told yourself about you or someone else.

"To err is human, to forgive, divine."
Alexander Pope

CHAPTER 2

Grounding

Your walk on this earth connects and transforms the hearts of those who are open and receptive. Your presence is infinite, only your form changes. Thank you for existing.

Álvaro Luis's Shoes

My son Álvaro Luis was such a loving and compassionate being! He valued and protected his family unconditionally. He enjoyed life immensely. He loved roller coasters and skydiving, adored travel, adventure and music. He loved architecture, languages, magic, gastronomy, philosophy, psychology; he truly loved the whole world and especially his family. He was very daring and risky, especially at extreme sports. His favorite poster, which I still keep next to me, was that of a boy walking a tightrope from one skyscraper to another in New York City.

I still remember, as if it were today, when I asked him why he took pictures of his shoes because it seemed very strange to me and he said, "Mommy, because I like my new shoes very much." Who would have imagined that the photo of his shoes was going to be a legacy for this book? Thank you, my son, for your walk on this earth. It is precisely your steps that have opened my eyes to understanding how much damage being disconnected from Earth has done to our society.

Grounding or Earthing

In the documentary film *The Earthing Movie*, directed by Josh and Rebecca Tickell, the damage that the use of rubber-soled shoes has done to human beings is clearly explained: rubber creates an insulating layer, and we lose the equivalent of the ground wire; we are exposed, without protection, to all the electromagnetic energy (EM) that surrounds us, which is extremely harmful.

The documentary also shows us how we can heal our bodies simply by walking barefoot on the ground; this charges us with antioxidant electrons and helps us put out the flames of inflammation throughout the body. Inflammation is the root of virtually all diseases. If we are barefoot, in contact with the earth, our body immediately absorbs minerals and antioxidants; it happens so fast that it is almost impossible to measure it.

In the film, we see inexplicable cases of healing, people who heal just by having done *grounding* or *earthing*.

Let us try to connect more with the earth (the sand, the rocks, the grass) by putting our entire body in direct contact with it, not just the feet.

My father, during his last months of life suffered a deep depression. He constantly said, "I want to die." I was very sad and urged him to take off his shoes and walk on the soft grass in his garden, but he replied, "No, my daughter, no, because I will catch a cold, and that will give me the flu." Now I understand that my father was completely disconnected from the earth. This is a perfect example of the disconnection that we human beings can suffer.

My son invites us to take off our shoes.

It is unbelievable that something as simple as finding the time and space to walk barefoot, has become so complicated. There are, however, other ways to connect with the earth naturally, not just by walking without shoes, although that's the best. You can also touch your pets, if they are grounded, that is, if they walk on the ground and not only on marble or concrete floors. If this is not possible either, there are even mats, cushions and patches for *grounding* that you can purchase online. I recommend earthing or grounding, in whichever way you can, at least fifteen minutes a day (preferably thirty).

My son's essence has invited me to be aligned and to connect every day with the elements of nature: air, water, fire and earth. In my opinion, our disconnection from nature has contributed, in large part, to the current chaos on the planet.

I remember my professor Tommy Rosen one day commenting that by watching someone walk, you can realize how connected to the Universe they are.

Nature

"Look deep into nature, and then you will understand everything better."
Albert Einstein

It is recommended for our optimal health that we spend at least four hours per week in contact with nature. In order to balance the body, mind and spirit, you must make it a priority to be in contact with nature. This has been crucial in my recovery.

Plants, trees, flowers and soil help us understand both the sacred and scientific worlds. Since my son moved to another plane, my connection with the environment has intensified. On many occasions, I have felt my son's presence in nature.

One day on his birthday, for example, his father and I were walking to dinner and came upon a majestic white fox in the Colorado mountains. It looked at us intently for a long time, motionless. It was very close, just a few steps from us. We got goose bumps and felt absolutely connected with Álvaro's essence. Later we mentioned it to the local residents, and they told us that there were no white foxes there. Then I searched online and read that they are already extinct in the USA and only live in Antarctica. In inexplicable situations like these, I confirm my son's presence.

When his soul had just been released and we went as a family to the retreat that he could not make it to, in northern Florida, a family of bears crossed us on the road; I felt chills all over my body because Álvaro had a bear as his WhatsApp profile picture, and when you asked him why he had that photo, he would say, "My spirit animal is a bear."

On another occasion, a gorgeous red bird, a cardinal, was on a branch out in our front yard. I was arriving from the airport, and when my husband opened the door, I told him to look at the beautiful cardinal. He spontaneously exclaimed, "That's Álvaro." Minutes later, with all our home's doors and windows closed, the cardinal was atop the fireplace, next to Álvaro Luis's photograph.

I could go on and on writing about many other situations in which I have felt, without a doubt, the connection with my beloved son through nature. I know he will always be present.

"If you can't see God in all, you can't see God at all."
Yogi Bhajan

It is essential to be connected, not only with the earth and the elements, but with others, with ourselves, with our inner self.

Addiction

My son's departure motivated me to study and read hundreds of books on healing and recovery. I finally came to understand that addiction is the disease of disconnection. If I had to define addiction with just one word, it would be that: disconnection.

"Addiction does the exact opposite of what connection does. Addiction tears apart, tears apart friendships, tears apart marriages. It will tear apart family, tear apart a whole community. Part of the reason we relapse is because of pain. There's some kind of pain that's in a lot of us, or all of us. We just don't want to feel anymore. And the further we fall into addiction, pain says to us, hell, we'd be better off just feeling nothing at all. So, we go numb. And our souls go numb. Now we've got a real problem. You know, pain is just pain. Not good, not bad, just part of being a human being. And sometimes good can come out of it, and if we are willing to go a little deeper, work our way through it, try to overcome it, well, we just might find our better selves."[2]

This is the monologue Dr. Finnix, played by Michael Keaton, delivers at the end of the *Dopesick* miniseries. It clearly illustrates the danger of disconnection and how related it is to addiction.

Disconnecting from our pain, from ourselves, from our friends and family, from the earth, leaves us totally exposed and vulnerable to addictions.

We seek to consume all kinds of products, including chemical substances that distract us, that prevent us from feeling, because we like to avoid pain. To feel is to heal, but our society has given us the message that crying or feeling pain is not good and should be avoided.

Having read both Dr. Carol Clark's book *Addict America* and Tommy Rosen's book *Recovery2.0,* I have understood that we are all addicted in one way or another; addictions to chemicals such as alcohol

---

2   Dr. Samuel Finnex played by Michael Keaton, *Dopesick,* directed by Danny Strong, Hulu, 2021.

and drugs are the most dangerous ones of course, because they shorten our lives on this plane, they take over our will, but there are many other types of addictive behaviors.

In America we are living a culture of excess, of constantly seeking entertainment; a society that is based on escapism. Addiction, as we already said, is the lack of presence. We are present when we are connected to our body and our inner self, only then can we connect with life.

My favorite definition of addiction is the one my teacher Tommy Rosen gives in his book: "Addiction is any behavior you continue to do despite the fact that it brings negative consequences into your life."[3]

The first time he asked us during a course to raise our hand if we did not have any addictions, I of course raised mine; one automatically thinks of drugs or alcohol. But he explained to us, as he does in his extraordinary book, that there are six great addictions, the big six addictions:[4]

---

3   Tommy Rosen, *Recovery 2.0: Move Beyond Addiction and Upgrade Your Life* (Author's Republic, 2022).
4   Rosen, *Recovery 2.0.*

- Drugs
- Alcohol
- Food
- People (codependency, sex)
- Money (gambling, debt, shopping, overspending)
- Technology

I have to accept that technology is an addiction for me. I still remember the day my son said to me, "Mommy, you look for your phone like I look for my pills." I also remember the day I was about to climb into the tub for a relaxing bath and realized I had the phone in my hand.

Coffee and carbohydrates are also strong addictions in my life. I recognize, too, that codependency is part of my life because I want to save others and make them happy.

Franciscan priest Richard Rohr of the Center for Action and Contemplation believes that religion may be an addiction for some; he works with many people to support them in their recovery.

I have also observed how people become addicted to soap or hand sanitizing gel. In truth, whatever your addiction or that of your loved ones, the steps to get over it are the same: do the inner work and feel (to feel is to heal and to heal is to feel once more). No one can do this for you, it must be you.

If none of the big six addictions resonate with you, Tommy Rosen explains, then it is necessary to evaluate the four aggravating behaviors because, even though nobody craves them, they are addictions as well, according to the definition, because one continues to repeat them even though they bring negative consequences into our lives. They are thought addictions:[5]

1. Negative thinking

2. Self-doubt

3. Procrastination

4. Resentment

We all have at least one addiction or aggravating behavior. What are yours? Ask yourself the question and dare to overcome them, one by one. I trust that the tools that have helped me will serve you as well.

Some of mine are my obsession with making everyone happy; my obsession with solving problems for others; my obsession with giving and gifting. It

---

5   Rosen, *Recovery 2.0.*

has taken me a while to understand that when I do what is right for me, it is right for everyone else.

The right thing for me, for example, is to complete this book even though my mind justifies every distraction that jumps up every moment. Procrastinating or postponing the completion of this book is an aggravating behavior; so, many times, I prefer to distract myself with other more pleasant activities that are irrelevant.

I also recognize what a bibliophile I can be, I buy books non-stop. I am a compulsive shopper, always looking for the cure. This also disconnects me and gives me only temporary satisfaction.

As I mentioned before, technology is also a big challenge in my life just as it was for my son. Today I realize that the planet has become ill, the opioid epidemic devastated the lives of my son and many other human beings, and the COVID pandemic came to impose stillness on us, to give us the opportunity to stop and observe all that we unnecessarily consume, to pay attention to our breathing and our anxious mind. Our planet needs us to wake up and take responsibility for the way we are and act. The evolution of the human race is no longer optional. Everything that we are going through is for the good of humanity, for our Mother Earth and the Universe.

I have no doubt that my son freed his beautiful soul to return to his Divine origin.

My son's soul will live forever reminding me that staying connected to the earth will be the sure way to be protected.

"We are spiritual beings having a human experience."
Pierre Teilhard de Chardin

Codependency

Codependency is losing oneself by being too busy taking care of others; for many of us it is easier to focus on others than on ourselves.

I want to talk in depth about codependency because this is what happened to me in relation to my beloved son. During my healing process, I have learned that in order to detach myself from code-pendency, the first thing I have to do is direct the light or lamp, figuratively, toward me in order to stop seeing others and observe how I am acting—to concentrate only on myself.

My son left me his light to illuminate the fact that we are the only ones responsible for our own lives, no one can save another person, you can only save yourself. My level of consciousness when Álvaro was alive was such that I still thought I could save, relieve or rescue my son from his addiction. That codependency with him made me get sucked into a cycle in which I could only give. It was difficult for me to receive. Codependent relationships become unilateral relationships.

Many times, we seek happiness outside of ourselves because we are not comfortable within our inner self; we look inward and don't feel good enough, successful enough, smart enough, or safe enough. So, then we look outward in our pursuit of happiness. This, in part, we learned from our parents.

Today I can understand that loving without knowing how to do it can hurt or cause harm to the people we love. It is imperative that a person feel free (rather than trapped) when they are loved.

Forgive me, my son, for being so overwhelming, intense and extremely tough when communicating. I was not aware of all of this at the time; it is only today that I can see it clearly. My emotional and desperate frame of mind did not aid in calming your anxiety or transmitting peace to you in any way.

Learning to set boundaries is essential; it is the basis of the work for recovering from codependency.

Thinking, worrying, and talking only about the problems of others prevents you from taking care of yourself and enjoying your own life. The need or desire to control others makes us unhappy. You must let go, lovingly. It is very important to understand that when you do the right thing for yourself, you are doing what is right for everyone.

Happiness is within us, although finding it sometimes involves hard work. Nothing that comes from outside will make us happy, only our inner work.

I really like the following phrase that has to do with addiction to people, that is, codependency: "I help more when I help less."

Many of us, as parents, have a hard time understanding that our mission is not for our children to always lean on us, but rather for our support to eventually become unnecessary to our children.

I feel that the healing of codependency can be summed up in the famous Serenity Prayer:

"God, grant me serenity to accept the things I can't change, courage to change the things I can, and wisdom to recognize the difference."

I remember that Álvaro was obsessed by *The Game* by Neil Straus. At times I thought that the book was negatively affecting his life, and I confess that one day I threw it away, only to discover very soon that my son had bought another copy. Álvaro believed in the methods explained therein which taught how to be better at seducing and conquering women. It made me suffer to think that the book exerted such a strong influence on my son's behavior because I felt that it led him to act less authentically and that it generated beliefs that made him suffer.

The belief system we have causes most of our suffering. Believing that we are not good enough is an example of the toxic voice that causes us to feel shame. Almost all addictions are deeply rooted in some type of toxic shame that makes us believe we are flawed or a mistake.

Our beliefs act as magnets in our life. For example, believing that the world is safe and supportive will attract situations, people and experiences that align with such beliefs.

Beliefs are usually formed during our childhood and are anchored in our unconscious; we resort to them to deal with our fears. Many are limiting, though, and they prevent us from living an abundant and fulfilling life.

As is clearly seen in the case of religion and politics, beliefs can unite or separate people: believers, non-believers, Jews, Muslims, Catholics, Protestants, Democrats, Republicans . . .

It is liberating to know that I have a consciousness that thinks, feels and has bodily sensations, but that is not who I am today. I choose not to waste time identifying with my thoughts since they have no permanence.

To live without beliefs is to encounter life in the present moment.

"A thought is harmless unless we believe it. It's not our thoughts, but our attachment to our thoughts, that causes suffering."
Byron Katie

Emotional Intelligence

Emotional intelligence, according to psychologist Daniel Goleman, who popularized the concept in 1995, "capacity for recognizing our own feelings and those of others, for motivating ourselves, and for managing emotions effectively in ourselves and others."[6]

Goleman identifies five basic abilities of emotional intelligence: discovering one's own emotions and feelings, recognizing them, managing them, creating one's own motivation, and managing personal relationships. This kind of intelligence cannot be measured, in contrast to IQ which can.

People who have emotional intelligence find that their relationships with others flow, they know how to put themselves in the shoes of others and feel for them. Being emotionally intelligent also involves taking the criticisms one receives as something positive because they are analyzed and learned from.

Having emotional intelligence enhances one's ability to be happy and also provides the necessary qualities to face adversities and setbacks with more resilience. In general, those people endowed with emotional intelligence enjoy learning new things continuously, are firm when required, always look forward, flee from monotony and look for alternatives to live a fuller and happier life.

My son's emotional intelligence was a challenge during his lifetime. My son Álvaro had an extremely

---

6 Daniel Goleman, *Emotional Intelligence: Why It Can Matter More Than IQ* (NY, NY: Random House Publishing Group, 2005).

high IQ, he was a brilliant and creative being, however, his learning difficulties and his attention deficit (just like mine) affected him in all areas of life. I believe that his level of emotional intelligence did not help him deal with a difficult and complicated illness such as addiction.

The mind is like an antenna, and unfortunately, my son's connected via technology with all the remedies and substances that help to block pain. The society and culture he lived in (our society) led him to think that pain can and should be avoided, although pain, as we have already seen, is part of life itself. By resisting pain, it becomes something stronger because, as we know, that what you resist persists.

His pain is my pain. This book invites us to connect with our own pain, to experience it fully without resisting, and to use the techniques and tools toward which Álvaro's spirit guided me in order to heal and grow.

I am grateful to have received them, and this acceptance prevents my pain from turning into suffering.

"Pain is inevitable, suffering is optional."
Buddha

I have learned that it is important to be humble and accept that one does not cause the addictions of loved ones, does not control them and does not cure them. They do however open up opportunities for us to seek paths of spiritual growth and to make us more compassionate.

Some people can use drugs and alcohol without becoming addicted, but others, without knowing or planning it, only by socializing and imitating others, get sick and become dependent on substances. The question is why are some people more vulnerable to chemical addictions than others? I feel, after my personal experience, that the sensitivity, creativity and learning differences of my son Álvaro Luis were factors that predisposed him to the disease.

Decluttering

In addition to shopping being an addictive behavior, the accumulation of clothes and objects that results as a consequence, disconnects us from ourselves.

Decluttering or clearing and organizing is necessary in order to uncover our essence. Thanks to my son I understood that it is crucial to remove everything that hinders or takes away power from our life, starting with the material or physical. It is essential to clean out all unnecessary objects from our saturated spaces in order to unlock energy, so that it flows, and so that the space is more harmonious and allows us to evolve. Understanding the importance of clearing my life in all aspects has been fundamental to be able to listen to my inner self.

The phrase "Less is more," which was made famous by minimalist German architect Ludwig Mies van der Rohe, is, to me, the perfect inspiration for getting rid of the superfluous. Identifying those things that we must let go of to lighten our luggage, is essential to open up space for abundance and a life with more freedom.

My nature, like that of my son Álvaro's is to keep it all; we collect cards, books, magazines, papers, advertisements, everything. We like to accumulate clothes, shoes, decorative objects, all kinds of artifacts and souvenirs. I've had a hard time understanding that the things I accumulate are actually distractions that keep me from getting into myself.

Every day, I strive to free my spaces because I know that to make magic happen in my life, I must open up free space. The very useful question I ask myself when I am decluttering is if I would buy the item I am evaluating again. If I wouldn't, then why have it?

I understand today that to uncover our essence it is a must-not to think that we are what we have, or we are what we do, but to realize that we are only who we are being in the world, that is, how kind we behave, how honest, loving, responsible, cheerful, grateful, adventurous and collaborative we are.

Álvaro Luis was an extremely loving and sensitive human being; he was afraid to feel and that is why he self-medicated with painkillers. He got sick with addiction and the whole family along with him because addiction is a family disease; it doesn't occur in isolation. Today I am somewhat grateful for the disease of addiction because it has made me evolve, become a more compassionate and spiritual human being.

My son lived a short life, yet he left us deep messages that will last more than a lifetime.

I thank my son for his art, which reflects and transmits the messages of his heart, of his love for life and the earth and thereby creates happiness for humanity.

Epigenetics

I really like the simple and clear way Dr. Eric Berg DC explains the fascinating field of epigenetics on YouTube. He says that genetics would be the equivalent of the music score, and epigenetics would be the interpretation, the way the pianist decides to play the notes. Epigenetics, then, is the environment in which we grow and live, and it can weigh more than genetics.[7] This is very hopeful because it shows us that we can influence our own DNA, that it does not determine us.

We can positively influence our genetics through:

- Healthy and nutritious food, as well as the time we eat and the speed at which we do it.

- Movement, exercise and posture of the body.

- Temperature; both cold and heat.

- Restful sleep.

- Stress and recovery.

- Laughter and humor.

---

7 "What Is Epigenetics: In Simple Terms – DNA Sequencing – Dr.Berg," Dr. Eric Berg DC, YouTube, September 3, 2019, https://youtu.be/g12kIu9jrIk.

- I would add these two more:
- Loving and positive thoughts.
- Meditation and prayer.

Epigenetics shows us that neither fate is marked by our DNA, nor genes are set in stone. It seems to me that the debate between nature or nurture is comparable to this one between genetics and epigenetics.

We write our own script daily by making the decisions that can impact our lives.

I feel that our society is fortunately becoming more aware each day of how nutrition affects our overall health. Until now, the health care system has been primarily focused on caring for the already sick, rather than building health from the base (sick care vs. health care). This is due to companies' financial interests, especially pharmaceutical companies.

Pain has opened our eyes, made us wiser. Now I understand how important it is to consider nutrition as an essential part of our lives in order to recover and feel optimal.

My process of making peace with food is still in a developmental stage, and I need to work a lot, making changes to my diet one day at a time. My son needed it, too.

CHAPTER 3

Mindfulness

Living in the present moment increases our health and well-being. Being stuck in the past or the future prevents us from flowing in harmony. Being present is the way.

Vintage Car on Lincoln Road, Miami Beach, FL

"If your presence doesn't work, neither will your word."
Harbhajan Singh Yogi

Living in the present moment increases our health and well-being. Being stuck in the past or the future prevents us from flowing in harmony. Being present is the way.

In this chapter, my intention is to share with you everything my son taught me to be more present in our lives.

Mindfulness

The opposite of addiction is presence; we heal by being aware and connected to the present moment.

A month after my son was released from this plane, I began my two years of training as a mindfulness facilitator. Today I know that this was a fundamental gift for my recovery. Educating my mind with intention and discipline has been a wonderful treasure that I will always value and continue to do year after year.

When the mind is where the body is, there is no suffering.

Dr. Jon Kabat-Zinn, founder and director of the Center for Mindfulness in Medicine, Health Care, and Society at the University of Massachusetts, defines mindfulness as:

"Awareness that arises through paying attention, on purpose, in the present moment, non-judgmentally."[8]

If we could do this, not all the time, because that is almost impossible, but at least most of the time, we would be able to calm the mind and live with more inner peace.

The practice of mindfulness can be formal or informal. The formal way would be through meditation. By meditating, we concentrate on our body, on our breathing, and in this way, we manage to connect with our inner self. We pay attention on purpose, as Kabat-Zinn says, only to the present moment, and without judging anything.

Mindfulness is liberating; while practicing it, I realize that I am not the voice in my mind, but rather that I am the one who listens to and observes that voice.

---

8   Jon Kabat-Zinn, "Mindfulness-based interventions in context: Past, present, and future," *Clinical Psychology: Science and Practice 10*, no. 2 (2003): 144–156, https://psycnet.apa.org/doi/10.1093/clipsy.bpg016.

Sharon Salzberg, one of the first people to popularize meditation and mindfulness in the United States during the '70s, points out that mindfulness helps us realize how we cling to pleasurable experiences and run away from those that are unpleasant.[9]

To practice mindfulness, you just need to observe how the mind gets distracted and flees from the present moment. We observe it, non-judgmentally, and bring it back (sometimes up to ten times or more per minute). The goal is not to stop our waves of thoughts, but rather to learn to ride them. It is a simple but not easy practice. I want to share with you the fundamental elements of the practice of mindfulness that I have learned from several teachers.

You have to be present:

1. Without judging.

2. With patience.

3. With a beginner's mind (stop being the expert).

4. With confidence.

5. Without striving to heal or restore.

---

9   Kabat-Zinn, "Mindfulness-based interventions in context: Past, present, and future."

6. With openness to free yourself and heal.

7. Anchored in the breath in order to let go and allow things to be as they are, without forcing them.

8. With gratitude and generosity.

Life is very fast paced; we have way too many appointments, to-do lists, excessive work with not enough rest, and technology that absorbs us. Sometimes we walk sleepily through the day, just reacting, without any conscience, and then our actions are not graceful or elegant. If we train ourselves to be aware through mindfulness, we will be able to better understand our inner self, and thanks to this, we will act (instead of just react) better. Mindfulness helps us to see things as they truly are and to build resilience in order to be able to respond skillfully to anything that comes our way.

The mindfulness backbone is patience: patience to learn to be observant without making judgments. Mindfulness allows us to treat fear and anxiety with love and compassion. Through this practice, the heart, body, and mind are integrated.

Many times, I invite my clients to put their hand on their heart to feel or listen to its beat, and when they have told me, "I do not hear it," then I tell them to try to find it in their pulse. "I still do not hear it," they tell me. Then I guide them to look for it on their neck until they finally feel it with their hand or fingers.

Wherever you are now, in this moment, I invite you to stop for a few seconds and find the beat of your heart. When you feel it, you can count the beats during inhalation and those during an exhalation, you will see that through this practice you are easily able to anchor yourself in the present moment and generate a space of peace and tranquility.

Listening non-stop to the ideas, thoughts, and stories of my mind all the time makes me nervous and fills me with anxiety. It is proven that we all have between sixty and seventy thousand thoughts a day and that most of them are negative, repetitive, and from the past. When I learned this fact, I knew that unless I could get out of my mind for a few seconds or minutes throughout the day, I wouldn't be able to listen to my heart, calm down, or live with inner peace.

I decided then that moving forward I would frequently put my hand on my heart to calm down and be grounded and prepared for anything that might come my way.

This practice is extremely helpful during stressful situations—when I am on a plane and there is a lot of turbulence, for example, or during landing or takeoff. It also works for me when I'm losing patience with my kids, partner, or boss; I look for a space and connect with the heart. Before making important decisions, doing interviews, or giving a lecture to the public, I always find the space and time for this practice.

I invite you to put your right hand frequently on your heart and connect that way with your breath in order to have more and more moments of inner peace.

Surely someone who sees you will ask if you are okay. I always answer, "I am very well, thank you, and more connected with my heart every second."

When we listen to the mind and not to the heart, we can make wrong or foolish decisions. Yogis say that when the mind and heart are not connected, we have a monkey mind, and it is the ego that dominates us. St. Teresa of Avila called the mind the madwoman of the house; Dr. Richard Hanson calls it the puppy, because it has to be disciplined[10]; and

---

10   Rick Hanson, *Hardwiring Happiness: The New Brain Science of Contentment, Calm, and Confidence* (NY, NY: Harmony, 2016).

my son said it was a wild horse because it would run amok and not let go of him.

Today I am grateful to have understood that it is possible to train and discipline the mind with the help of mindfulness and breathing.

What physical exercise does for your body, meditation and breathing do for your mind. Did you know that there are gyms for the mind where you can go to meditate and breathe in a group? I invite you to give them a try.

"You practice mindfulness, on the one hand, to be calm and peaceful. On the other hand, as you practice mindfulness and live a life of peace, you inspire hope for a future of peace."
Thich Nhat Hanh

Movement

We have all experienced some type of trauma, which develops when we fail to process our painful experiences fully, and thus, they remain stored in our body, specifically in our cellular tissues. Hence the phrase "the issue is in the tissue" that I heard from Professor Nikki Myers, addiction expert and founder of Y12SR (Yoga of 12-Step Recovery). We can, however, unlock and release all kinds of stuck trauma at the cellular level through various forms of conscious movement and body work. We can even shake them out of the body, just as animals do instinctively.

Movement is one of the things that helps us stay present.

The first physical activity I turned to in order to recover, after accepting that I would no longer be able to physically touch my beautiful and lovely son, was the game of tennis. In addition to the great benefits of moving, I received many hugs from my teachers and the lovely women with whom I play. They literally nourished my soul with their hugs!

Later, when my body aches subsided, I was invited to dance, and I discovered a magnificent therapy in Zumba and African dance. Conscious movement has a miraculous effect; it helps us recover because movement is the song of the body, and it is one of the things that helps us stay present.

> *"One thing that can solve almost all of our problems is dancing"*
> *James Brown*

Dancing helps us manifest what is going on within ourselves.

The spark of life begins with movement, it is our first form of expression and, therefore, we can use it to ignite feelings when we are going through dark moments.

Álvaro Luis, my son, enjoyed dancing immensely; he took classes in Miami and NY and danced wonderfully. I still remember one day that I visited him in the NY apartment he shared with his roommate, and he gave me a demonstration. He put on a video of Sven Otten and Parov Stelar and imitated the dancer to perfection. Rivers of sweat were dripping on his body: he was amazing, and it really moved me! All the time I kept discovering more of his talents. His sensitivity and creativity were prodigious. My son was not his illness, he was an extraordinarily talented being.

In my personal life, physical exercise has been essential. Completing eight half marathons helped me cope with the stress of addictions. The best medicine for my recovery has been walking, playing tennis, dancing, jumping, yoga, biking, running. Movement heals.

I am convinced that one is as young or old as one feels and that our flexibility is a fundamental part of that feeling. If our back is stiff when we are twenty, we will be old at a young age. If, on the other hand, at seventy, our back is still flexible and mobile, then we will continue to be young. Our nervous system, in addition, depends on how energy circulates or flows through the spine. That's why I want to share with you these exercises, inspired by Kundalini yoga, that I practice every morning to stretch my spine and keep me flexible and young.

These are the eight movements I do daily. You can see them in this YouTube link.

1) Sitting cross-legged on the floor with your spine straight, place hands on your knees and gently rotate your body clockwise. Inhale as you move forward, and exhale as you move back. Breathe in and out only through the nose. After at least eight circles, rotate in the opposite direction for at least eight counts. Treat your body with kindness, respect it and go at your own pace, without judgment.

2) Sitting cross-legged on the floor with your spine straight, hold your shins and flex the

spine by expanding your rib cage as you inhale and go forward, then contracting it while exhaling and gently moving backward. Do at least eight times. Repeat with hands on knees instead of shins.

3) Sitting cross-legged on the floor with your spine straight, place your hands on your shoulders, breathe in and twist to the right. Breathe out while returning to center. Breathe in and now twist to the left. Breathe out and return to center. Do this at least eight times, always looking straight at the horizon.

4) Shrug your shoulders like when you were little, raising and lowering them, taking away the responsibility and shaking off the burden of the world. Breathe in as you pull them up and out as you lower them.

5) Rotate your head as if drawing a circle with the tip of your nose, be very slow and gentle as this is the cervical cord. Do eight neck rolls to the right and eight to the left.

6) Opening yourself up for victory, raise and extend your arms until you form a V, then fold at elbows and bring them down. Inhale while rising and extending, exhale on the way

down. Go at your speed, as vigorous as you can, but with kindness and respect for your body. Smile.

7) Stand up with heels together. Gently bend forward and place your hands on the floor. If you can't reach the floor, use yoga blocks or a chair. Bend knees, then extend. Inhale up, exhale down. Do twenty-six frogs, as my teach recommends, or as many as you wish.

8) To finish this morning routine, hug yourself, close your eyes and feel the energy you have created in your body. Be thankful for the goodness that this morning routine will bring to you throughout your day, and if you'd like, give yourself a kiss on the top of each shoulder.

The Power of Hugs

In her book *Touch*, Dr. Tiffany Field explains the importance of physical touch, both for our healthy development during childhood, and for physical and mental health as adults. Physical contact is as decisive to our health as diet and exercise.[11]

All the hugs I received after losing my son made me understand firsthand how much they help one to heal, so I decided to invite an extraordinary group of people to give free hugs on the streets of Miami Beach. The experience was captured on YouTube. I invite you to see the campaign and the public's response. To this day, it continues to bring love and recovery into my life. Simply looking at it makes me feel my son's love.

---

11   Tiffany Field, *Touch* (A Bradford Book, 2003).

When psychiatrist Juan Carlos Paredes hired me to work with some of his patients as a life coach, I took the opportunity and asked him if he had information in his medical library that scientifically proved the wonderful effects of hugging and physical contact on mental health. I am very grateful to him for the numerous studies he shared with me. In short, a hug helps us be more present, opens our heart, connects us with our feelings and our breathing, strengthens our immune system, balances the nervous system, diminishes stress, and increases oxytocin and serotonin, the hormones of happiness.

As Dr. Tiffany Field explains in her book, the physical contact therapies that exist today and are recognized are divided into three:[12]

Energy methods

- Acupressure
- Acupuncture
- Reflexology
- Tai Chi
- Yoga

---

12   Field, *Touch*.

Manipulative methods

- Chiropractic work
- Therapeutic massages
- Osteopathy
- Trager method, which involves movement of muscle tissue

Amalgams

- Tactile therapies, which include both energy and manipulation therapies
- Chinese massage (combining massage and acupressure)
- Polarity therapy
- Reichian massage
- Feldenkrais technique
- Applied kinesiology
- Amalgamated therapeutic massage, created by the "Touch Research Institute" directed by Tiffany Field

In her book, Dr. Field mentions Jim Burke, former chairman and CEO of Johnson & Johnson, who highlights the importance of touch in disease prevention. He says he has no doubt that people who have been well-loved from birth to death have fewer illnesses. He says that he would even bet all he owns on that, and that he is sure science will develop models that suggest that we can strengthen the immune system through contact.[13]

Importance of Posture

My son worked with a coach who singled out just focusing on body posture in order to feel better. When we are told that all we have to do to feel better is think positive, we know that it's not that easy. But understanding that there is a connection between our thoughts, emotions, and body posture helps.

If we try to consciously observe and improve our body posture and our facial expressions, we also automatically influence our emotions and thoughts. Since the emotional state of the body is the environment in which our cells live, if our body is loaded with negative emotions, we can get sick, and vice versa: postures that are conducive to positive thoughts help us to avoid diseases.

An empowering posture, for example, is to stand with your back straight, stretching it as much

---

13   Field, *Touch.*

as possible, your shoulders back and relaxed, your chest slightly forward and up, looking proud, your chin raised and your eyes forward. I invite you to try it: take a deep breath, relax your eyes and forehead, hold the posture for sixty seconds and notice the difference you feel. Your mind listens to your body, and that's why your posture is a wonderful tool for your restoration.

When we smile, we send a message to the brain that we feel good, and then the chemicals and endorphins that are produced generate a high vibration. Even a forced smile can help us for this effect, and in case it cannot be forced, a horizontal pencil can be placed in the mouth and that trains us, in some way, to smile.

If, when we walk, we think and feel that the soles of our feet are kissing the earth, this helps our posture to be enhanced.

Deep breathing is vital to achieve a relaxed posture, I will talk more about breathing in the next chapter.

Music Therapy

Another way to be present, to connect with the current moment, is through music.

Álvaro Luis always loved music. As a child he learned piano with a South African teacher who adored him, and when he went to college, to Xavier University, he learned to play guitar like a professional. I regret not being able to record it so I could continue listening to it. My son was fascinated by attending all kinds of concerts, as a family and alone; he liked rock, techno, and classical music: all genres. He had the opportunity to do community service at Jackson Hospital in Miami, invited by the great leader and music therapist Pablo Landi, who treated people who arrived by air ambulance after having wanted to take their own lives; he helped them align their energy fields and chakras through vibrational healing techniques with tuning forks.

For a long time, my son carried drumsticks in his backpack and used them continuously.

Expressive Arts Therapy

This morning, at 4 a.m., a paper mâché puppet that Álvaro Luis made when he was only twelve years old, dropped all of a sudden from my cabinet . . . And then I felt the need to wake up and write about art therapy.

My son, like many other people, had a hard time talking about his feelings, so self-expression through art was wonderful for him.

Expressive art therapy is a therapeutic modality that combines psychology and the creative process to promote emotional growth and healing.

A therapist or counselor will suggest a form of art that best suits us for exploring our outer and inner world through the use of our senses. It is not necessary to have experience or training in any of the art forms; what is important is the creative process itself through which you will focus on and release specific problems and difficulties.

Some of the many forms that can be used in expressive art therapy are:

- Playing music or listening to music
- Writing lyrics
- Theater or improvisation
- Reading or writing poetry
- Journaling
- Storytelling
- Reading or writing fiction
- Drawing

- Painting or fingerpainting
- Sculpting
- Dancing
- Life maps, videos, memory books

All these forms of expressive art can help us to communicate our life stories and heal from traumatic experiences by working through them.

For my son's essence, it was extremely important to explore art; it helped him to stay present and connected. His teachers recognized his talent and sensitivity. However, the socio-cultural perception of his school and society in general placed much more importance in sports, and it was not *cool* to be artistic. Today I am aware of the role that art therapy can play in helping people of all ages to connect with themselves and recover. I think a fine arts college might have been ideal for him.

Laughter

Álvaro Luis's sense of humor was exceptional, his favorite comedian was Jerry Seinfeld, and on the day of the third anniversary of his departure, Álvaro Luis's brother ran into him. These are the ways in which my son's spirit continually manifests itself to us.

Laughter is like a protective weapon, a gift that we have as humans; it lifts our spirit and makes us more resilient; it oxygenates us, rejuvenates us, and helps to release stress. It anchors us to the present moment because when we laugh, we are not thinking about anything, we are not worried about the past or the future. It can be a vehicle for developing the habit of happiness in your life. It helps as a catharsis of those emotions that one has been carrying for a long time.

We can relearn to laugh fully, train the body to do it with our diaphragm, as we do naturally when we are babies, because many times due to society, lack of humor and cultural beliefs, we limit ourselves and cut laughter in half.

For the body there is no difference between laughter with or without reason, that is, both spontaneous and programmed laughter have benefits.

Cardiologist Dr. Miller of the University of Maryland prescribes his patients one of those belly laughs that draws tears per day, because those laughs generate nitroxide, which massages the arteries and heart.

Sitting down to watch a funny video, spending time with friends or family that make us laugh, doing a laughter yoga class or a laughter therapy session to learn to laugh for no reason, all of these help release endorphins that contribute to our mental and emotional well-being. On a psychological level, laughter increases self-esteem and self-confidence. Laughter therapy works as brain gymnastics and helps us manage stress better.

Laughter should be taken seriously because, like tears, it oxygenates and cleanses our body inside. Laughter is health, and health is life.

"A day without laughing is a day wasted."
Charles Chaplin

Our well-being depends on the balance we achieve between our body, mind, and spirit. Laughter, movement, music, art, mindfulness, and physical contact play an important role in our lives because they help us achieve this balance.

"In the end, just three things matter: how well we have lived, how well we have loved, how well we have learned to let go."
Jack Kornfield

Tapping (EFT)

During my last visit to the jail before the pandemic, I was able to bring some copies of books on tapping as a gift for the prisoners. It was wonderful to teach them the technique and guide them to experience its benefits.

I first learned about tapping, also known as EFT (emotional freedom technique), during my visit to The Sanctuary at Sedona, a healing center in the state of Arizona, which I consider to have the most complete holistic and integral program I found during my journey to heal my son.

Tapping is an energy-balancing, stress-relief technique that uses both Chinese acupressure and psychology principles. It focuses on the specific meridian or energy points in our body that will be tapped with one or two fingers (you can also choose to tap with your fist or your whole hand) while stating the stress or frustration that is being felt at the moment. It is recommended to use your own words to be more effective.

Tapping works because stress and emotions are felt in our whole body, and when we think about them in a relaxed state, they do not have the same power over us, and so it is easier to let go of them and become more balanced.

We start by looking at the negative first, we look at our problems first, and then we clean it with positive statements. We learn to master our mind and create the life and the thoughts we want.

A statement example could be:

"Even though I have this problem (describe the problem), I totally love and accept myself."

The statement with the problem is repeated while you tap all the acupressure points.

The key to all this work is to be honest.

Tapping was first made known and promoted by Gary Craig in the nineties. Today, Dawson Church, who I was very fortunate to meet, is a big presenter of EFT. There is also an annual summit organized by the Ortner family where many promoters of this technology give testimony of its multiple benefits. There are scientific studies that prove that tapping helps to renew brain wiring.

The most typical acupressure points to tap are the following:

1. Karate point or side of hand

2. Base or start of eyebrow

3. Side of the eye or super eagle eye

4. Underneath the eye

5. Underneath the nose

6. The chin (the crest between lip and chin)

7. Collar bone

8. Underneath your arm like a hand away from your armpit (bear hug point)

9. Top of the head (monkey point)

Some people end by grabbing the wrist of the opposite hand.

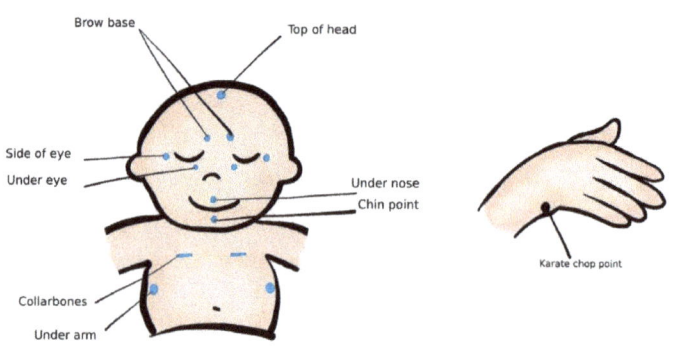

We can choose any hand or any side of the body or both sides at the same time. I choose to tap approximately eight times on each point for five minutes daily.

The tapping will send calming signals to the amygdala, which then generates changes in the mind. It releases cortisol (the stress hormone) improving our health by helping to regulate emotions.

Many people use this technique to achieve greater productivity and focus, others to have more abundance or to improve their finances.

Before you start the tapping exercises, it is recommended to do some deep breathing and ask yourself how intense your stress around the issue you are working with is, from zero to ten. After the tapping, at the end, ask yourself again and compare.

Access for free our exclusive video to heal your heart.

Discover 8 simple exercises that I practice daily with my loved ones, empowering me to open and connect with my spine. I sincerely hope they contribute to your journey as well.

Join our mindful community and participate in future events!

chateodelcorazon.com/giftvideo

CHAPTER 4

Breathing

*Focus your attention on your inhalation and exhalation,
observe your thoughts, and let them go.
Repeat, and you are meditating.*

The Clouds

During one of the many classes I taught as a volunteer in prison, a very kind, young African American, about the same age as my son Álvaro Luis when he died, said to me: "Teacher, this breathing that you just taught me makes me feel the same as I felt with the drugs I was consuming." I explained to him that we have an inner pharmacy and that breathing has the potential to make us *high* without hurting us. "It is your power and the greatest treasure to obtain your freedom even while inside prison." At the end of the class, he approached to ask me if he could give me a hug.

My greatest and most debilitating fear was not being able to heal or free my beloved son from addiction. I was constantly anxious, and breathing was the only thing that could anchor my mind. Today I can affirm that, thanks to God, I no longer fear death, and I know that Álvaro Luis will live forever in our hearts, through his work and his messages. His spirit manifests itself very often in our lives, the only thing that is no longer here is his physical body. I have faced fear and anxiety with kindness and firmness, finding a little healing and recovery each day; I accept without judging and understand that progress is what matters, I do not seek perfection because not only is it impossible to achieve, but trying to obtain it only generates frustration.

Wherever you are right now, I want you to know that no matter how hard what you're going through or what loss you've had, there's a way to get your heart back and be happy again.

The first psychiatrist who worked with my son was an expert Kundalini yoga teacher and he would say, every five minutes, "breathe." At that moment I did not comprehend the depth of his words, and in my monkey mind, I asked myself how I could be paying so much money for someone who would only say "breathe," as if it were a magic formula. It seemed to me that specific, targeted medicine (amphetamines) and natural supplements would be what would heal my son. It took me a long time to find the experts who talk about the healing power of breathing and be able to feel its effectiveness, which is, in fact, almost like a magic recipe. Nowadays when I feel fear, I use my breath to anchor my mind.

My ego self makes me think that I would have liked to know back then that there was a complete science that explains how the simplest and easiest thing, breathing, can heal a person. Science explains how breathing changes and activates the nervous system and the hormonal system. My limiting belief was that this was too simple to be true.

In so many visits to psychiatrists and hundreds of specialists, breathing was no longer mentioned to me, until I went with my son to Omega Institute in New York where the psychiatrist, who was also a shaman, helped people heal through rebirthing breathing. My son did not agree to participate. I understand now that he wasn't ready to heal, which was immensely difficult for me to accept. I focused on doing my own job, which was to stop being obsessed with healing him. I believed that healing was going to come from the outside; I did not understand that it is only from within that we can achieve changes in our lives. It was necessary for me to be able to empty myself and breathe consciously, only breathe, for Grace to come into my life. It was necessary to let go of *doing* and *having* in order to simply *be*.

Learning how breathing influences our health has been the greatest learning and gift derived from the illness of my beloved and precious son Álvaro Luis.

There are entire books on the different breathing methods that exist, there are different schools of teaching, teachers, scientists, healers, shamans . . . And yet, very few allopathic doctors observe you or ask you during their consultation about how you breathe.

Holistic doctor Andrew Weil, a Harvard graduate, says that the first question he asks his patients is how they're breathing, and the second one is how much water they drink a day.[14]

I'd like to share with you some of the multiple breathing techniques that have accompanied me in my own recovery and that I have been able to share and experience with a wide variety of students, including prisoners who are doing time, serving their sentence. Inside prison, prisoners can learn to have inner freedom through breathing: even enclosed within four walls, they may feel free. Aren't we all doing time?

I invite you to explore these and many more techniques on your own.

It is important to know that, if when practicing the following breathing exercises, you feel dizzy

---

14   Andrew Weil, *Spontaneous Healing: How to Discover and Embrace Your Body's Natural Ability to Maintain and Heal Itself* (NY, NY: Ballantine Books, 2000).

or faint, you should stop immediately and return to your natural breathing rhythm. Practice without pressure.

"Breath brings you life. Each breath, as it comes, is a true gift. Pay attention to it as it comes into you. When you can feel your own breath ushering in life, it brings comfort and fulfillment."
Prem Rawat

Breathing Exercises to Relax

1. Clouds Exercise (5 min)

As you inhale, imagine how clean air enters your mind and body and when you exhale, imagine that it is expelled as dark and black, releasing all tox-  ins from the body and mind. This is a process of cleansing mind and body.

2. Alternate Nostril or Soothing Breathing

In meditation posture, cover your right nostril with your right thumb and inhale slowly and deeply. To release the air, cover the left nostril with your index finger, uncover the right and expel it through the right nostril. Repeat the same thing on opposite sides. The left orifice, according to yoga is the channel of feminine and lunar energy; it calms us and cools us, serves to free us from anxiety and anger. The right nostril is the male and solar energy channel; it helps us focus.

3. Diaphragmatic or Abdominal Breathing

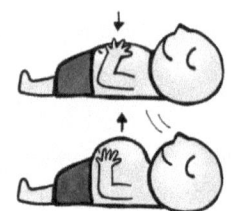

The benefit that this breath has is psychological, it has been described as "nature's own sedative" because it has a calming effect and helps body and mind to achieve a state of balance. It is an invitation to use our lungs' full capacity. Place your hands under your ribs or on your abdomen, inhale deeply through your nose and allow air to push your hands up and lower them as you exhale. If we observe a newborn baby, this is his normal breathing. Long, deep breathing expands and elevates consciousness.

4. 4-7-8 Breathing

Exhale and empty all the air from your lungs. Inhale slowly through the nose for 4 counts, hold your breath for 7 and exhale for 8 counts, through your mouth. Repeat four times. This is Dr. Andrew Weil's favorite breath; it helps reduce anxiety and is very effective for falling asleep.

5. Bee Buzzing

Place your tongue on the upper palate, where the teeth begin, and make a buzzing sound like bees. At the same time cover your ears with your thumbs  and use the remaining four fingers to cover your eyes, thus closing all windows to outside sensations and helping you concentrate on feeling the buzzing inside your head.

I do it for a couple of minutes two or three times a day because, just like humming music, it increases nitric oxide in your body fifteen times. Nitroxide ensures the proper functioning of our body.

6. The Cube

It helps us focus, re-lax and it is easy to teach to children.

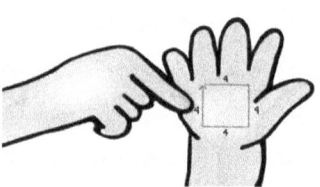

On the palm of your hand, trace a square with the index finger of the other hand. Start by inhaling and count-ing to four while you trace the line up. Hold your breath for four counts while you trace a line across, to one side. Exhale for four counts while you trace down. Hold your breath for four counts while you trace the bottom and close the square. Repeat the steps as many times as you want.

7. 7/11 Breathing

Start by inhaling for seven counts and exhaling for eleven. Note that the exha-lation will be longer than the inhalation.

This breathing exercise is very special for me be-cause my son weighed 7/11 when he was born.

8. Breath of Fire

This is an invigorating and purifying breathing technique. This breathing is done through the nose, with your mouth closed. The important thing is that the spine is straight; you  can be sitting or lying down. Inhale through your nose as you inflate your abdomen and exhale forcefully through your nose as you completely deflate and contract your abdominal muscles. Inhalation and exhalation should last the same amount of time, and there should be no pause between them. To better understand this, some yoga teachers ask their students to imagine and imitate the breathing of a dog while it is panting, but with your mouth closed.

This breathing is a tool against anxiety, nerves, worry, fear, pain, and sadness. It helps with depression and detoxifies the body, boosts your immunity, and increases vitality. (If you're pregnant or on your period, this breath isn't for you right now.)

I have learned that healing begins with and depends on the breath. If we take the time to learn to breathe, recovery from any circumstance in life will be much easier and better.

All addictions come from a feeling that something is missing. When we feel that lack, we breathe poorly or superficially, sending a signal to every cell of the body with the message that our main need is not being met, that something is missing. Then the patterns of tension arise in the body and mind. People who suffer from addictions (all of us, really) usually breathe partially, hurriedly, and superficially.

Breathing through the mouth is not recommended and yet a large percentage of people do so. Having heard the recommendation from several experts to wear a Micropore 3M strip to sleep, I decided to try the suggestion, and it was amazing to wake up feeling extremely restful.

I feel that when I breathe correctly, I connect with my soul, and from there I can feel love. Creating from the space of the soul, I can evolve into the best version of myself. Now I understand why the Kundalini expert professor would repeat over and over "Breathe" as if it were a magic recipe. It is.

Actually, we could conclude that breathing can be considered the new science of a lost art.

I invite you, from this moment on, to stop several times a day to observe how you are breathing and to try one or more of the breathing exercises that I have shared with you.

The Door to Your Freedom Is in the Breath

As mentioned above, I have learned that the vast majority of people who suffer from substance addictions breathe inadequately. My son had a blockage in one of his nostrils. He wanted to have surgery so he could breathe better.

Breathing is our first and greatest gift in this life; it is our primary form of nourishment, and it is the gateway to our freedom; it is up to us to understand and harness it. We can silence the mind through breathing, breaking the incessant cycle of thoughts and feelings.

It has taken me a long time to understand that something as simple as breathing can be such a powerful channel of healing and recovery. Of course, even though breathing is simple, it is not easy to pay attention to it, to do it with intention and dedication.

Our breath is the barometer of the internal state of our being; that is, the breath is the mirror of our mind. Our thoughts and feelings are reflected in how we breathe. Anything we do or feel affects our breathing, either positively or negatively. And vice versa, if we breathe consciously, we can positively influence our mood. When you breathe deeply and completely, your body relaxes and releases tension, increasing oxygen in your body, which makes all your systems work better. Deep, full breathing balances the nervous system and lowers the heart rate. Finally, natural, deep breathing gives us a different perception of life.

The Healing Power of Breath

In many countries and traditions, the word *breath* has a greater meaning than merely the physical.

In India, the word *Prana* means air, physical breath, but at the same time it is also the sacred essence of life.

In traditional Chinese medicine, the word *Chi* means life energy, cosmic essence and also the natural air that enters our lungs.

In Japan the word *Ki* means presence, will, mind or breath. *Ki* is extremely important in martial arts and spiritual practices.

In ancient Greece the word *Pneuma* meant air or breath and also spirit or essence of life.

The *Kahunas* (*hunas* means "secret") or ancient priests of Hawaii used breathing exercises to generate spiritual energy called *Mana*.

Since ancient times, breathing has been regarded as a crucial link between nature, the human body, mind, and spirit, and yet today most of us do not give it enough importance, and hardly any doctor asks you how you breathe.

Breathing to Calm Your Mind

Breathing in your life is essential and safe, however, the practices of some breathing techniques can exacerbate certain medical conditions, so I ask you to consult with your doctor before practicing any of the exercises that I have shared with you.

In *Becoming the Iceman*, a book written by Wim Hof and Justin Rosales, the authors say that it has been scientifically proven how through the power of breathing people can change their lives. It explains that we have the ability to control body temperature and that through extreme cold and our breathing, we can connect with the deepest parts of our mind.[15] When we feel intense cold, we stop thinking, overriding our limiting beliefs.

Nowadays, in many universities (Wayne State University and Radbound University, among others), his life (Iceman) and the scientific power of his method are studied. Countless lives have changed thanks to his practices with breathing. Hof invites us to modify our psychological paradigms, makes us question whether it is possible to connect with what makes us happy, strong, and healthy, and the answer is that it is possible! When we feel bad, without strength and without health, if we practice breathing in the recommended way, we oxygenate the body, raise its pH for a minute or two and restore the brain; we thus penetrate our mind's thoughts. Wim Hof's goal has been to scientifically prove how breathing changes people's brains and lives. I recommend his book or his website, https://www.wimhofmethod.com/, to those interested in exploring his methods.

You are the alchemist! To access the magic of internal physiology, you inhale deeply and let go, in-

15   Wim Hof and Justin Rosales, *Becoming the Iceman* (Maitland, FL: Mill City Press, 2011).

hale deeply and let go, you stop after exhaling, and you concentrate on feeling, because feeling is the way to heal and for you to go straight to the heart, to stay in the present, without thinking.

If we breathe deeply and completely, we will achieve the following results:

1. Relax the body and release tension, achieving better absorption of oxygen in each cell.

2. Increase the body's oxygenation, which creates energy and improves functioning of all systems, particularly immune, muscular, endocrine, digestive, nervous and cardiovascular.

3. Balance the central nervous system, stimulating the parasympathetic.

4. Lower heart rate and blood pressure.

5. Increase the levels of oxygen entering the brain, which will give us more clarity, concentration, and strength.

6. Calm and focus the mind.

7. Lower stress hormones (cortisol and adrenaline) and with this, strengthen the

immune system, helping to heal and re-cover.

8. Achieve control of the mind to be able to guide our thoughts. Breathing is the foundation of many spiritual practices.

Walking as Free People

"Whenever your mind becomes scattered, use your breath as the means to take hold of your mind again."
Thich Nhat Hanh

During my experience as a volunteer in prison, I have been able to share teachings of other teachers, such as those of this beautiful Buddhist monk who very recently let go of his body and who recommended that we walk as if we were kissing the earth with our feet. I share with you, and I suggest you practice this exercise of the great master Thich Nhat Hanh.

When I walk, I inhale and take two or three steps, I pronounce the name of a loved one, that of someone who can bring me a feeling of freshness, compassion, and love. I pronounce their name every time I take a step. If I despair, it is because I have fed my despair and then I must focus again on my breath and walk as if kissing the earth with my feet, with serenity.

Thich Nhat Hanh says, "If I am depressed, the Buddha recommends that I thoroughly examine the nature of my depression to determine the source of the food I use to nourish it. Once I determine the source of the nutrients, I have to stop them, and the depression will go away in a week or two."

Without full awareness in my daily life, I feed my anger and despair by looking at and listening to very toxic things around me. Living consciously means ceasing to ingest toxic material that harms us. So, I decide to stay in touch with what is wonderful, renewing, and healing in my environment.

During the first facet of my recovery from the loss of my son, what helped me cope the most was listening to body scan meditations. I remember one specifically from Davidji, and one from Dr. Elisha Goldstein. Today as a mindfulness facilitator, I lead my clients in their personal scanning. Most TV programs and series have plenty of very toxic material; it is important to filter what our minds receive.

Later I regained the strength to begin meditating. When I empty my mind, I feel how the soul of the Universe fills me with its breath. Life is fragile and unpredictable; I feel very grateful for meditation and mindfulness because they have helped me to accept life as it is and not as I want it to be.

"To meditate is to listen with a receptive heart."
Buddha

CHAPTER 5

Morning Habits

Your powerful, loving spirit inspires the whole world to have compassion. You planted peace in our hearts and taught us to accept things as they are.
Thank you for your light!

Miami Beach, Florida

I thank my son for waking me up to live a more spiritual, conscious, and fulfilling life. I thank him for his invitation to transform my limiting beliefs and also to observe my out-of-tune behaviors. I thank him for opening the doors of silence and meditation to me.

Gratitude is a practice that involves both body and mind; it is necessary to consciously stop paying attention to all external factors in order to generate stillness in our life and be thankful for it.

> *"If the only prayer you ever say in your entire life is thank you, it will be enough."*
> *Meister Eckhart*

Thanks to my son Álvaro Luis, I understood that the disease of addiction is a family disease: it affects each and every one of its members in various ways. Each member in the family has a role and a process to work on at a personal level, each one must understand that addiction is composed of physical, emotional and spiritual elements and that to overcome it, you need to work on all three planes.

I thank my teacher Tommy Rosen for helping me clearly understand that everyone has addictions in different areas of our lives. As I have already mentioned in the chapter on addiction, I am addicted to people, what is known as codependency. I am also addicted to technology. I get nervous when I do not find my cell phone; as my son said, "You look for your phone as I look for my pills." I also have food addictions, especially to cheese, coffee and sugar. I also realized that the way in which I buy books, without limit, is addictive.

Some addictions or dependencies do not risk or take our lives, however, as we know, there are substances including alcohol and drugs which do. It was the case with my son: he left too quickly and too young. The disease of addiction took hold of him, and he could not break free. Today I celebrate his life, love him, and honor him with this book. I appreciate his great collaboration in getting it written. I know that my son's spirit guides me and directs this recovery manual from another plane. Throughout my healing process, I have learned that energy is not created nor destroyed, it is only transformed.

Thanks to my son, I have found my purpose: to assist others in recovering from their losses and achieving a personal reconnection. I appreciate each of the messages I have received from Álvaro because through them I have been able to slowly restore my heart and to support others in achieving their own healing.

Thanks to his messages, I have been able to awaken my soul and understand that we all carry wounds or traumas; if we process and work on them, we can transform pain into wisdom. It is necessary to see the trash in order to be able to clean it.

Thank you, Álvaro, for inspiring me to develop a daily spiritual practice that has become the greatest treasure in my life; it has helped me live one day at a time and be able to generate a miracle every morning: the miracle morning.

I start each morning drinking a large glass of water with intention, and then I appreciate at least three or four things in my life, many times I seek to reach eight.

I am grateful to author Hal Elrod for inspiring me with his book *The Miracle Morning: The 6 Habits That Will Transform Your Life Before 8 A.M.* in which he explains the six elements that he considers necessary to transform our mornings into miraculous ones. Elrod developed this routine after having studied the practices for the development of success and awareness of multiple disciplines that have existed over the years.[16]

He wanted to know what the most successful people in the world do for their personal development and found that there was no one thing alone. He ended up with a list of six and wondered what would happen if he carried them out together, so he consolidated them into a ritual, to be practiced daily, and this routine has given rise to a great world movement of miracle mornings.

If you, too, want to create miracle mornings, follow the six-step morning routine using what he calls life SAVERS: silence, affirmations, visualization, exercise, reading, and scribing.

Miracle Morning

Waking up before 8 a.m. is the secret.

1. Silence

2. Affirmations

3. Visualization (as we will see in Chapter 7)

4. Exercise or movement (as we saw in Chapter 3)

---

16   Hal Elrod, *The Miracle Morning: The 6 Habits That Will Transform Your Life Before 8 A.M.* (London, England: Teach Yourself, 2018).

5. Reading

6. Scribing

I recommend that you practice each of these steps for five to ten minutes. However, as Hal Elrod tells us, even devoting a minute to each of these activities has enormous benefits.

- I take the liberty of adding two more elements that have made a big difference to me:

  1. Start with a green juice every morning.

  2. Finish your shower with very cold water, increase the seconds you spend under very cold water little by little.

Silence

"Silence is a source of great strength."
Lao Tzu

I still remember when a friend said to me, "Claudia, you could never do a yoga class because you don't know how to be silent." That made me realize that what I needed most was to start a yoga class in order to start creating small spaces of silence in my life, and to learn how to look inward, dare to witness my interior. Learning to be silent every day has been a big challenge for me.

Many times, when we try to be silent, our mind overwhelms us with its noise; however, once we understand that our thoughts are just like passing clouds and we learn to observe them without attaching ourselves to them, to let go and let them go, we can be at peace, in silence, and learn to listen to our heart instead of our mind.

A simple way for me to achieve a state of silence is through the observation of all my senses and body. Although really for me, prayer and meditation are the most powerful tools there are to be able to enter into silence and connect with the Universe.

As Tommy, my teacher, says, if we solve our inner world, the outer world will solve itself.

"Silence is peace,
Silence is solace,
Silence is love,
Silence is salvation,
Silence is nature,
Silence is life,
Silence is gesture,
Silence is vibes . . ."
Namramita Banerjee

"Listen to the silence, it has so much to say."
Rumi

Affirmations

Affirmations are a powerful tool for programming and reprogramming our mind in a positive way. They are statements that we can repeat out loud or in silence in order to reinforce that we are capable and deserving of achieving what we want so much in our lives. Affirmations must be positive, in the first person, in the present tense and as if they were already a fact.

Part of my personal recovery has included connecting each day with some of the affirmations I have in my books, cards, and calendars. I like to write them on a piece of paper and stick them on my mirror. I say the affirmation, I feel it in my heart, and I share it with the world.

Affirmations help us create new thought patterns that align with our true desires.

I want to share with you the following eight affirmations I have learned on The Insight Timer App, from Mark Guay that have personally been very useful to me.

1. Everything I need to live a full life is with me now or is on its way.

2. Every day I feel more empowered thanks to my skills and talents.

3. I believe in my abilities, and I am worthy of greatness. I believe in my abilities and deserve to succeed.

4. I love who I am and see challenges as opportunities to grow and be stronger.

5. I speak with confidence and surround myself with people who empower me.

6. I follow my own path and tune in to the higher source that guides me.

7. I embrace change, seek full happiness, inhale courage, and exhale fear.

8. I trust and know that the best part of my life begins right now.

These affirmations are said at the time of my daily morning meditations. The first thing I do is invite a possible affirmation. One of my favorites, by Emile Coué, which I repeat twenty times every morning is:

"Every day and in every way, I am getting better and better."

If you are interested in affirmation ideas, I share one of my favorite ones daily through Instagram. You can follow me here: @chateodelcorazon.

Reading

"The more that you read, the more things you will know. The more that you learn, the more places you'll go."
Dr. Seuss

Reading has been a great challenge in my life because, although the greatest virtue for me is the love of learning, it was difficult for me to read, and I used to fall asleep very easily as soon as I started reading.

One day, however, I read that a very good idea for reading more and better was to organize a reading group. So, I managed to motivate myself to invite some good friends who loved to read, and we created a group that today, after thirty years, we still have. We get together and enjoy reading together while sharing life itself.

Now I have become a bibliophile; I search for ideas of healing and wisdom in books. I am very selective and sometimes I go directly only to the chapters that interest me. Audiobooks have been wonderful to me because one can read while driving, cooking, cleaning the house, or playing sports. Reading is food for the mind. It helps us to improve memory and concentration, to be more open and to make better decisions; it allows us to understand the perspective of others and thus to have more empathy. For all this and more, creating the habit of reading in our life is indispensable.

"Reading is to the mind what exercise is to the body."
Joseph Addison

Scribing or Writing

Writing as a healing tool is formidable, but it needs to be practiced daily. The goal is to put our emotions on paper; write in a simple way without worrying about creating a work of art. It's just about taking a pen and a notebook that inspires you and writing down your emotions as they come to you.

My second son gave me a journal with philosophical questions, one to be asked in the morning and one in the evening, all in order to develop my wisdom. I like it a lot because it inspires me to think openly and write more easily.

Journaling helps us record our emotions and thoughts and better understand why we feel this way or that. Writing every day has many benefits, especially when we are stressed or anxious.

I share with you three different ways of organizing a writing journal.

1. Bullet diary.

2. Write and develop short, simple, and accurate ideas.

3. Lists of objectives and projects that we want to achieve.

I am grateful for the disease of addiction in my family for having opened my heart to learning about so many alternative therapies, programs, gurus, healers, experts, teachers, guides and specialists who have enriched me and helped me understand that in order to heal my soul I had to center it in my heart. This has been my spiritual journey. I have to say, though, that centering or sitting my soul in my heart has taken a lot of work because it likes to get up every minutes, so I have to use a sense of humor and say "sit" many times.

I thank my Twelve Steps godmother for always telling me that I need to dig deeper.

I thank addiction for opening me up to understanding human vulnerability and to be more compassionate.

I have learned to feel inner abundance and to name the things for which I am grateful each day. I have also learned to visualize the things I want to happen in the future and to be thankful for them in advance. Our brain doesn't know the difference between what's real and what's imagined, so if we imagine something as if it's already a fact, we attract it more easily.

Being grateful generates high, positive feelings, and science has shown that this improves our health and helps us live happier lives.

I thank my beloved son for guiding me to feel more and to understand that all human beings fail to accept and forgive the human condition. I have learned to be more vulnerable and humbler. If we learn from our mistakes, we awaken the compassionate observer we all carry within us.

My son used to make us very happy with his cooking. Food was a great pleasure to him; he liked to share it with me and the whole family. He cooked for us like a great chef, and you could see he really enjoyed it. He had a beautiful smile and smiled daily . . . It was incomprehensible to me that inside, in silence, he was enduring the pain of addiction.

Thanks to Álvaro, I discovered the strong connection between food and addictions. My son loved sweets as much as I did, and I know now that sugar is the gateway drug to all other drugs.

Californian Dr. Julia Ross, author of *The Mood Cure*, has a recovery program for addiction based on nutrition and supplements. My son attended the program, and as a family we practiced it for a while. I remember how complex it was to organize at least twenty bottles of different supplements to take each day.

I thank the Universe for having been chosen your mother and through your eyes to have captured so much beauty. I feel very fortunate to have had the privilege of feeling so much love by your side. Every day I discover many more of your messages. Every morning when I wake up, I am grateful for all the light you send me so that I can see things with love because that is what you are: pure love.

I remember when you were five years old and you asked your grandmother, "Grandma, what is love?" Your grandma remained quiet, and you insisted, "Do you know or don't you?" Actually, you were and are pure love. I also remember the day I was planning the party for your First Communion (you were only seven years old), and I was worried about the clothes to wear, and you told me, while patting your heart, "Mommy, that's not important, the important thing is here."

I also keep your favorite phrase, by Eleanor Roosevelt, close to my heart:

"Great minds discuss ideas; average minds discuss events; small minds discuss people."

Son, you are in me, and I am in you, thank you for being my teacher.

Ho'oponopono

There is an ancient Hawaiian ritual that Dr. Ihaleakala Hew Len, PhD, used with psychiatric patients and that thanks to Joe Vitale, through his book, *Zero Limits*, became known. This book explains the powerful ancestral technique called ho'oponopono that has to do with the fact that we are all connected. Its fundamental practice is that we take responsibility, one hundred percent, for everything that happens in our lives.

To solve all our problems we must trust, clean, restart and rewrite.

To do this we repeat:

"I am sorry.

"Please forgive me.

"Thank you.

"I love you."

We make this request mentally and let it flow through us; we leave everything in the hands of our Higher Power. I invite you to look into it more deeply when you have a chance because it is a very powerful practice.

CHAPTER 6

Gratitude

Nothing happens by accident. We are where we need to be right now. We must trust and focus only on becoming the best version of ourselves.

Times Square, New York

My sons have aunts who live in New York and when Álvaro was seventeen and his brother fifteen, they invited them for a visit. I didn't give them permission, but they still ran away for a weekend to party. That trip marked the beginning of my son's love affair with the city that never sleeps. He became obsessed with its art, buildings, music, and food. With the support of his dear aunts, Álvaro had many opportunities to visit it before moving to live there during a few years of college.

New York was the world of his dreams where he was happy and able to blend with the outside world. As I mentioned in another chapter, he learned to dance swing like Sven Otten, he imitated him perfectly; he learned to play guitar in college, and listening to him was a great honor and privilege. He didn't like to play in public. He was a shy boy, and I feel that what bothered him the most was getting attention.

Álvaro Luis loved to laugh; he loved Jerry Seinfeld; he was fascinated by film and TV. Friends admired him for his intelligence and sense of humor. He conquered everyone with his conversation, he possessed the gift of the word. He fought only with me because I knew of his weak point, and he saw his reflection in his mother's mirror.

Álvaro Luis's life on this plane was short, but his presence is infinite; he broke free from the complex disease of addiction and became an angel to his family, and a hero to me because in every moment I feel his protection. Since he left his body, we, his parents, and siblings have come together and led a more authentic and spiritual life. Every day as a couple we work our miracle morning, and our marriage of almost forty years has been strengthened immensely: our son Álvaro Luis gifted us with a somewhat heavenly union. We are so honored and thankful to have been chosen as parents of a son who lit up our lives and taught us to feel and live life with compassion. His passage through this earth was very brief to the human eye; however, his footprint and his teachings are extraordinary and eternal. He deeply touched the hearts of his beloved family, friends, and an immense community, leaving us great messages and learnings.

My son came to invite the world to connect with everything beautiful and wonderful that exists in order to recover health and well-being and to teach us how to be happy and get to be the best version of ourselves.

Each and every one of us, as we go through this earthly life, just as Álvaro Luis did, will leave a legacy behind. That is, a spiritual heritage, ideas, or traditions that we transmit to the next generation. Everything we need in order to do this is with us now, or on its way.

I invite you to think about what you want to leave as your legacy to the younger generations.

My father, for example, left us his creativity and his love for culture and art, specifically classical music and opera. He was a very loving man who adored his family, had strong religious beliefs and a great passion for news and politics. His love for education led him to be the founder of the Technological University of Mexico, which today is the largest private university in the metropolitan area of Mexico City. His orderly and disciplined life, his loyalty to his friends, his sense of humor and his honesty are his powerful legacy. He also loved sports, and his daily exercise discipline influenced me greatly. My father left a great mark on my life that I value and appreciate immensely.

I think it is very important to ask ourselves what the motto that our elders left behind for our family is. The motto left to me by my family of origin is "Education and musical culture make your life happy."

Happiness

"Happiness is when what you think, what you say, and what you do are in harmony."
Mahatma Gandhi

I am very grateful for having stumbled upon via-character.org, an organization where I learned about the eight virtues that help people be happier, and that I share here with you:

Enthusiasm "Zest"

Rise opening your arms to the sky, animated and with lots of energy and vitality, ready to face the day with great encouragement and rejoicing. Let's do it!

Hope

Believe that the future will be better than the present. Have faith.

Gratitude

Take the time to express appreciation for what you have and for what you want to have. Be aware of the good things that happen to us and be grateful for the joys as much as the challenges.

Gratitude is a virtue that helps us transcend.

"Whatever you appreciate and give thanks for will increase in your life."
Sonaya Roman

Curiosity

Discover and explore different subjects and topics that bring wisdom to your life. Be curious because knowing is enriching and makes us better.

"Let your curiosity be greater than your fear."
Pema Chodron

126

Love

Love begins with the kindness that I practice with myself.
When I accept my imperfections and my disorder, I begin to love myself.

"You're a person worthy of love. You don't have to do anything to prove that."
Sharon Salzberg

Value your relationships, especially those that are reciprocal. Share with and care about those who are close to you. Take care of relationships that empower you and know how to let go of those that don't.

"True love is eternal, infinite, and always like itself."
Honoré de Balzac

I add three virtues I feel are essential to find joy after loss.

Courage

It takes a lot of courage to cope with pain and struggles. You have to be brave to speak out with conviction, even if you stop being popular, and also say what is right, even if there is opposition.

Fear is keeping you from reaching your potential. Conquering fear I feel is the most important goal in life. We experience fear because we are human. Moving from fear to excitement is the key of courage. I like to substitute saying I am afraid for I am excited. Courage empowers all virtues. Feel fear and do it anyway.

"Courage starts with showing up
and letting ourselves be seen."
Brené Brown

Wisdom

Wisdom is prudence that develops through our life experiences. It helps us to order and judge everything we know. Wisdom provides us with sane judgment.

> *"Wisdom comes alone through suffering."*
> *Aeschylus*

Self-control

This is the virtue of moderation. It means having a strong character that helps us to control our thoughts and impulses. It is the discipline of our behavior. This virtue can be acquired with maturity or training; it is linked to good relationships, the best mental health and utmost academic performance.

The path to lasting happiness is not simple or fast; you need to do the work and accept the change because change is the only thing that is constant. Happiness depends on the development of your character.

I really enjoy working with young people because their energy is refreshing and sincere. The first question I frequently ask them in our initial appointment is whether they believe it is possible to be happy without drinking alcohol, and the second is whether they believe a family can be happy without toasting with wine or any other alcoholic beverage. Most of the times, young people tell me that they do not believe it is possible to live happily without alcohol; this way of thinking is ingrained in our society, our Western culture.

We seek happiness outside of ourselves, because within us we often feel uncomfortable. Maybe we don't feel successful or good enough, confident, or smart enough. We also seek happiness outside because we learned it from our parents. My father was addicted to buying classical music and opera CDs, and I am addicted to buying books.

It has really been very difficult for me to understand that alcohol and drugs are the same thing, that there is no distinction when it comes to recovering from addiction. Many times, I am ashamed for not knowing then that it was better for me not to drink alcohol in front of my son when he was going thru the difficult process of achieving sobriety. I forgive myself because I did the best I could with the consciousness I had at the time.

Recently, I was in my therapy with Dr. Sonpal, and she asked me why I still drank alcohol if this had been the reason why my son had gone to another plane. It took me a couple of weeks to answer myself. Now I understand that I continue to drink and enjoy a glass of wine from time to time because I am not addicted to substances. However, when I am with people who are, I no longer drink, to support them in the arduous task of recovery.

Today I know how difficult it is for people recovering from this addiction to live in a society where alcohol is at the center of all meals, gatherings, parties, and celebrations.

My admiration, respect, and complete support for all those beings who live one day at a time, freeing themselves from consuming substances in order to recover. I ask the Universe to support them and provide them with all the necessary strength to be firm throughout their process.

"Being alive is all you need to be happy."
Prem Rawat

It is common to think that we will be very happy when we have more money, but in reality, it has been shown that the richest people are not the happiest, and that, once the basic needs are met, one can be very happy. Swami Bagavatti says that expecting happiness to come from money is like milking a cow and waiting for orange juice.

Instead, there is a virtuous circle between happiness and generosity. The happiest people are the most generous, and being generous can make us happier. Being generous benefits us both physically and psychologically; for this reason it was very important for my son Álvaro Luis to volunteer in the community; he had many opportunities to do so and was very happy when he took them. It is important that when you need to ask others for help, you do so with the confidence that you are giving them the opportunity to generate happiness in their life.

Sometimes we think that being generous is more complicated than it really is; we believe that you need to invest a lot of time or money. However, it only takes small, simple acts of generosity. While it is true that there are those who have available time to visit organizations or centers and volunteer in person, it is not essential in order to be generous.

Some examples of simple acts of generosity are things like telling someone they do their job well or observing and recognizing positive qualities in others. Making someone laugh is also an act of generosity, or simply smiling, because our smile is the most generous thing we can provide. Another example may be to pick up trash that is not yours. Really listening to another human being, giving food to those who need it, visiting a sick or elderly person who is or believes that they are alone, all these are very simple gifts to give that will nourish both those who give and receive them.

> *"The best way to cheer yourself up is to try to cheer somebody else up."*
> *Mark Twain*

This phrase is wisdom from the past and also a part of the new science of happiness.

Kindness is contagious, and my son spread his to everyone around him. He was a very kind being; he donated a lot of his time listening very carefully to others. We were there together in both the good and bad times.

> *"We make a living by what we get.*
> *We make a life by what we give."*
> **Winston Churchill**

Acceptance

Accepting myself completely is necessary to be able to develop my new, enhanced version. It is indispensable to accept and love what is, and to understand that all failures are part of the journey. I must accept that I am perfectly imperfect and enjoy my process. If I fall seven times, then I get up eight, this is the way I can be resilient and brave.

> *"My imperfections and failures are as much a blessing*
> *from God as my successes and my talents*
> *and I lay them both at his feet."*
> **Mahatma Gandhi**

My son Álvaro's loss actually became a lesson for everyone; we all realized that in life you either win or learn; loss is not a reality. Álvaro continues to accompany us with his loving and protective spirit.

Nothing I would have done differently in relation to my son would have prevented his departure:

this has been the hardest thing for me to accept. As I mentioned in the introduction, my mind tricks me into thinking that if he hadn't been kicked out of the program he was in, he might not have died, that if I had picked him up or if he hadn't had access to an Uber app to go out searching for a drink, that if he had been in another program or in another country, maybe everything would have been different. Acceptance of things as they are is the hardest, but at the same time, it's the most important thing in order to be able to evolve and heal.

We personally experienced the huge opioid epidemic with my son Álvaro Luis: he lost the battle along with so many thousands of young people in the United States. Today we are living another epidemic, a pandemic through which many lives will also be lost. In my opinion, this gives us a great opportunity to do a sort of private retreat. That is, we can learn to connect in a more spiritual and conscious way in our life so that we can recover from the terrible battles we are experiencing. It is crucial to understand that, despite everything, we can choose to be happy no matter what. For this, we must learn to remain in the eye of the hurricane where there is only calm. We must take every situation that arises in our life as an opportunity to grow, evolve, and become a better person. If we take the time to process and work on any trauma or difficult situation that we have had to live, we will be able to become the best version of ourselves.

Life is an opportunity for everyone to write their song; that is, everyone has a theme and a mission in life and that is their song. The biggest challenge is to find your mission so that you can transcend. Each and every one of us comes to this earth with a purpose, and to find it, it's necessary to listen to our soul, which expresses itself with passion. We just have to stop our inner noise and listen to it.

CHAPTER 7

Visualization

*Your dreams are magic, build them
into your life with passion.*

St. Basil's Cathedral, Moscow

We had the wonderful opportunity to travel as a family to the island of Bali in Indonesia. My son knew that the plane would stop in Russia and asked if it would be possible to do some sightseeing; he was told that it was not because it would be very complicated. The surprising and extraordinary thing was that the flight he took with his brother made a long stopover in Moscow, and as if by magic, my son managed to spend a night in Russia as he had dreamed and visualized.

This mosaic created by my son represents the integration of his life from heaven to Earth.

Visualization

Imagination is a very powerful gift that all human beings have; it makes us unique. Experts and therapists who specialize in stress agree that imagination can affect us, both negatively, if we let it flow and generate fear and frustration, and positively, if we use it as a tool to achieve our goals and dreams and to improve our health.

Since the beginning of civilization, shamans or healers, Native Americans, Australian Aboriginal people, Hindu yogis, and the ancient Greeks have used visualization to combat disease.

Many personalities of recognized success say that visualization has played a very important role in their lives. Among them we can name Bill Gates, Oprah Winfrey, Anthony Robbins, Tiger Woods, Arnold Schwarzenegger, Jim Carrey, Will Smith and Jack Nicklaus.

Jack Nicklaus, the great golfer, confesses that he does not make any shots without first having a sharp and focused image of the shot. Jim Carrey, the actor in one of my son's favorite movies, *Dumb and Dumber*, wrote himself a check for ten million dollars in 1987, dated for Thanksgiving 1995. Under concept, he wrote down, "for interpretation services rendered." He continued visualizing it during those years, and in 1994, he was paid exactly that amount for his film.

Visualization can help us overcome habits that limit us and help us transform into an improved version of ourselves.

Through visualization we become director, producer, and actor of our own film; we create, produce, and act all the scenes.

Dr. Patricia Norris believes that there are four characteristics that make visualization effective:

1. It must be generated by oneself.

2. It must conform to one's own values and ideals.

3. All the images must have a positive tone.

4. It must be kinesthetic and somatic, which means that you must feel the physical sensations in your body: see them, hear them, feel them, smell them, and even taste them.

If we want to fulfill our goals and dreams, if we want to reach our greatest potential, it is essential to become experts and masters of visualization.

It has been scientifically proven that actually living an experience or just imagining it activates the same areas, networks, and neural connections of the brain. That is, your mind does not know the difference between what you imagine and what actually happens, so if you visualize it effectively, your mind encodes it as a real memory. For example, visualizing a sunset brings us the same effects of peace and health as sitting in front of the sea watching it.

Saint Ignatius of Loyola always recommended reading the Scriptures and visualizing yourself in each scene, joining them as if you were living them.

Visualization is an extraordinary and powerful tool for reprogramming our brain. The reticular system of the mind consists of filters that accept only the ideas that coincide with the program we are creating. Visualizing helps us reprogram neurons in the reticular system and train the mind to look through a different filter.

When you visualize:

1. Use all your senses, including emotions, sounds, sensations, and even use "special effects."

2. Participate in your visualization as a protagonist, not as a spectator.

3. Practice. We learn by repetition. Create the habit of visualizing daily, and if possible, twice a day. It is ideal to do it immediately when waking up and just before sleeping. You can do this together with your thank-you practice.

4. Try to visualize in great detail, so much detail that it takes you almost the same

time and effort to visualize it in your mind as to do it in reality.

5. Write it down so that you can see it on a daily basis.

There are several visualization techniques. I share some below so you can explore them and find out which ones you like, which ones work best for you.

Video

You can create a movie with images of everything you want to achieve in your life, including affirmations, music, and powerful emotions that inspire you. These images must show, in a detailed and specific way, what we want. They can show it as if we have already achieved it.

Track path

A set of papers and/or cards with positive thoughts, affirmations, ideas, and images that we paste along our daily path to remind us at all times of our goal.

Vision board or collage

A set of images of what we want to achieve cut out from magazines, newspapers, or printed from the internet, pasted on a table or cardboard, and placed in sight to help us remember what our goal is.

Script of your success

Another way to visualize is by writing a script that describes each step you have imagined you need to take to achieve your plans and dreams: describe the light, sounds, smells, what you are wearing, who is with you, what you hear, what you feel, how you live it . . .

Before you start, take a deep breath and have confidence in yourself. The better you visualize things, the more confident you will feel, and the more security you will gain for building new skills. One of the most important aspects of visualization is to get a real sense of how it feels to achieve your goals and objectives.

Some psychologists, such as Jung, Brewer and Freud, documented how some of their patients were able to cure themselves of some diseases through their imagination. Carl Jung gave the name "active imagination" to the mental process through which, in a state of lucid dreaming or state of relaxation, one consciously imagines and resolves the end of a recurring dream.

Active imagination is another form of visualization. My son Álvaro Luis consistently read a book called *Lucid Dreaming by Stephen LaBerge* that talks exactly about this.

Imagination, intuition, musical appreciation, and spatial awareness are functions of the right part of the brain and are therefore very valuable for dealing with stress.

Sleep

Sleep is critical to our health because that's when the body repairs, heals, rests, and grows. If you're not getting enough sleep, you're gradually wearing yourself out. It is said that we must sleep more to achieve more, because our body needs to recharge after each day to have a productive next day.

Sleep plays a crucial role in our immune system, our metabolism, our memory, our learning, and many other vital functions of the body. Through my son's process, I learned that all chemicals, including alcohol and drugs, greatly affect sleep, and the consequences are dramatic.

Studies show that only 3 percent of the population has a gene that makes it possible for a person to function well with only six hours of sleep a day;

the other 97 percent of us need on average seven to eight hours to restore our energy. Each of us should make a personal assessment of how we feel during the day depending on how much we sleep, and according to that we must determine our sleep needs.

It has been extensively documented that getting enough sleep allows the body to function at higher levels of performance. Not only do we work better and faster, but our attitude improves as well. Lack of sleep, on the other hand, generates lack of clarity in our thoughts, difficulties to concentrate, and sometimes problems with memory.

My son was not able to sleep the right amount of time; at times he slept more than ten hours but others he could not sleep even four. I still remember that one of the alternative recovery treatments for his addiction, with Ibogaine, that he was offered outside the United States, caused him the side effect of not being able to sleep for more than a week.

Álvaro taught me that determining the proper time of sleep we need, and sleeping that number of hours each night, is indispensable for health and well-being.

It is worth mentioning that sleeping too much is not good either. According to research done by the National Sleep Foundation in the United States, sleeping more than nine hours is associated with an increase in illnesses or accidents and also with higher mortality. Studies also found that sleeping more than nine hours can lead to depression.

Hal Elrod, the creator of the miracle mornings I have already told you about in Chapter 5, and who has significantly inspired my life, tells us that the way sleep affects our biology may be tied to our personal belief in how much sleep we need. That is, if I think I need to sleep eight hours to be rested and sleep only six, I will be tired; however, if I change my perception and before bed, I tell myself that six hours are enough, I will feel that they are.

Sometimes we are not aware of the immense power that sleep has in our life:

1. Sleep improves your memory. When you are sleeping, toxins are cleansed from the mind, the skills you learned during the day are consolidated and your memory is strengthened.

2. Sleep can help you live longer. Both over- and under-sleeping are associated with a shorter life; therefore, you have to sleep the necessary number of hours.

3. Sleep reinforces or increases creativity. Researchers at Harvard and Boston College found that while we sleep, the emotional components of our memory increase, which makes us wake up feeling more creative for any job we are going to perform.

4. Sleep helps maintain a healthy weight. Researchers at the University of Chicago found that people who dieted and were well-rested lost up to 56% more weight than those who were sleep deprived.

5. Sleeping makes you feel less stressed out.

CHAPTER 8

Purpose and Meaning

I ask the Universe to put me in the places it wants me to be, with the people it wants me to be with.

Tulips on Park Avenue, NY

"God, put me in the places you want me to be. With the people you want me to be with. Doing the things you want me to do. Thank you for the joys and challenges of my life. Amén."

The Recovery 2.0 Prayer of Tommy Rosen

I learned this beautiful prayer from my teacher Tommy Rosen, with whom my son Álvaro Luis was enrolled for a recovery yoga workshop in August 2015. He could not make it because he died on July 30. As I wrote in the introduction, his two brothers and us, his parents, decided to attend on his behalf. It was in that space where we first connected with his infinite presence; we felt and understood that Álvaro Luis had fulfilled his mission in this life and that he had come to save our family.

Álvaro Luis made us be more united than ever; he generated great strength within our family. Thank you, my son, for your infinite presence in our lives and for the messages you transmit to us daily.

A month before my son left, I was very happy because I felt sure that we had found, finally, the program that would save him. The ego kept deceiving me on a daily basis. It has been very hard for me to understand and accept that I can't save anyone, but I have understood it at last.

I can tell you, however, that even though Álvaro did not make it to the course, Recovery 2.0 with Tommy Rosen, it is definitely the most complete program I found for my own recovery.

Wim Hof's method of healing with ice water and breathing is also an extraordinary option that helps one emerge strengthened from all kinds of difficult situations.

I can assure you that whatever challenge you're going through at the moment, you can not only overcome it but also take advantage of the situation to grow and become the best version of yourself.

It is so true that what breaks our heart is also what connects us, so I thank my son for having opened a new path of compassion and understanding toward myself and all humanity.

Thanks to my son I have learned to live every day, one day at a time, creating miracles daily and flowing with the Divine will. Every day I make it a point to try to find the balance between my body, mind, and spirit. I've learned that the best way to predict the future is to create it myself, and for that I commit to doing the work one day at a time. I train my mind to meditate and to feel the emotions I want and need for my healing.

In the same way, I work daily on my connection with others.

Purpose and Meaning

"He who does not live to serve, does not serve to live."
Mother Teresa of Calcutta

Being kind to others makes us feel good. Altruistic acts have been proven to awaken and stimulate the same pleasure center in the brain as food and sex.

We come to Earth with a purpose: knowing what it is will give greater meaning to our life. Finding your own cause, something that is truly important to you and to society, will bring you happiness.

We all have unique and special talents and abilities that help us elucidate our purpose. If you haven't yet identified what makes you unique, I invite you to make a list of your skills and talents. If you have a hard time, ask someone very close to you, someone who values and loves you, to help you do it. When we recognize our talents, we can make sure we keep developing them.

Volunteering

"The best way to find yourself
is to lose yourself in the service of others"
Mahatma Gandhi

Practicing volunteering helps us find our life's purpose and make a difference in the lives of others. Using our skills productively connects us to the community while helping us develop new skills as well. Volunteering also aids us in our healing because to give is to heal.

Volunteer work gives us the opportunity to meet new, wonderful people and many times new friendships arise. As a mentor I can share what I know, but I can also learn from other perspectives. When we volunteer, we put the needs of others above our own and thus force ourselves to bring out the best in ourselves. Sharing our time, skills, and energy over and over again in the service of others shapes and develops our character, makes us better human beings.

Casual Acts of Kindness

During one of the programs I participated in with my son, I learned that to feel better and brighten my life, I could simply go out and practice casual acts of kindness, for example giving a flower or book to the people I met on the street. I would look them in the eye and say a word of encouragement to them; this practice has been an extraordinary experience in my life. I remember a time when, upon receiving a rose, a policeman's eyes got teary, and he expressed his love for his Heavenly Mother. When I feel discouraged or lacking in motivation, I try to go out and, with a clear intention, share a gift that benefits and cheers someone else.

Relationships

Álvaro Luis valued his parents' marriage very much. He spent a lot of time in our bedroom, studying our books and commenting on them with great interest; he gave me a few gifts, but one day he gave me a CD of *Never Gonna Let You Go*, by Sérgio Mendes; that was the song that my husband and I danced to at our wedding. He didn't know it, but his spirit did.

My son taught me that the quality of relationships is much more important than quantity, that all our relationships derive from the love of oneself, so loving yourself is not selfish, but rather the solution to improve all your relationships. This is because if we have a good relationship with ourselves then we can be better in our relationships with others.

I discovered that the secret is to become your best friend and stop wanting to make others happy or want to change them because you can only change yourself. You can only choose to love others, or not.

When I do what is right for me, it is the right thing for everyone.

Through the Twelve Steps program, I found a daily practice that helps me generate better relationships and that consists of asking myself the following five questions that I share with you:

1. What have I done today to show respect to myself?

2. What have I done today for someone else?

3. What have I done today to realize that nothing that happens is about me?

4. What bothers or irritates me today?

5. What am I grateful for today?

These questions have helped me a lot to boost morale and have greater confidence in myself.

Neuroscience has proved that healthy relationships improve our immunity and extend our lives. The good news is that the skills needed to create healthy relationships can be taught.

The work of best-sellers Dr. Helen LaKelly Hunt and Dr. Harville Hendrix, with over forty years of research, provides hope and teaches us to improve all kinds of relationships. They say that talking is the most dangerous thing people do, and that listening is what we know how to do the least.

This marriage of expert relationship doctors has developed a simple process, a first aid kit, to teach us how to have safe conversations; the most beautiful thing is to see them exemplify it themselves.

These are the five elements for achieving secure conversations. I invite you to practice them and to look deeper into their work.

1. Make an appointment

Ask if it's a good time to talk. We all have a movie in our minds we'd like the other to see, when we want; however, it is necessary to investigate how the other person's film is.

2. Mirroring

"Let me see if I understood you." Repeat what the other person said; this relaxes and regulates emotions.

3. Validation

"I have to make sure I understood."

4. Curiosity

Ask if there is more to say, make only positive affirmations (say nothing negative) and feel how the positive energy is contagious.

5. Summarize

"Let me sum it up." Ask if I have understood it well, without criticizing and without judging.

We must learn to speak; it's not what we say but how we say it.

It is important that the speaker and the listener look at each other's eyes and breathe three times in sync. At the end they will hug. Secure relationships release neurochemicals in the brain that create peace and calm.

I believe that the key to success in each and every human relationship is appreciation for the other, because when you appreciate, you are thankful, and it is gratitude for the other that enriches us. What we appreciate appreciates us.

I have learned to play the game of appreciation with my partner, my husband of thirty-eight years: at night before bed, we tell each other a couple of things that we appreciate about each other, and the next morning we repeat it. This intentional practice of appreciating your partner helps improve the quality of our relationships. To feel appreciated is to feel loved.

Each and every one of us expresses and experiences love differently, so it is important to identify the love language of our loved ones.

Gary Chapman, author of the book *The Five Love Languages*, says that each person expresses and receives love differently. Here are the five forms of love language he describes:

1. Words of affirmation
2. Acts of service
3. Receiving gifts
4. Quality time
5. Physical touch

I invite you to explore and identify the love languages in your relationships and discover which languages your loved ones value most. For my son, quality time and gifts were the most important things.

Some of us have families that add, contribute and support, but others have families that subtract, damage and complicate our lives. Whichever family you have, the important thing is to be able to recognize its influence and have the courage to set boundaries, if need be. When we are very young this can be difficult; however, it is very important, and the sooner we can recognize the influence that family has in our lives, the better.

> *"Open your mouth only if what you're going to say*
> *is more beautiful than silence."*
> *Arabic Proverb*

Neurolinguistic Programming (NLP)

I had the opportunity of studying a course on this incredible practice, made up of strategies and perception techniques that are easy to learn, and aimed to seek excellence at University of Miami.

Neurolinguistic Programming (NLP) analyzes the way our thoughts affect our behavior; it studies how our brain interprets the signals it receives and the ways these interpretations affect what we do. NLP is a technique that helps us guide our mind systematically so that we communicate what we think effectively. It studies intrapersonal communication (how we communicate with ourselves) and interpersonal communication (how we communicate with others).

NLP is art and science at the same time, its goal is to identify success and replicate it. It is a psychological approach that analyzes the strategies that successful people use to be able to apply them systematically to achieve our goals.

Neurolinguistic programming was created by Richard Bandler and John Grinder during the '70s in California.

The first NLP assertion is linguist Alfred Korzybski's phrase: "The map is not the territory," that is, that the information on a map is only a representation of the territory, not the territory itself, in the same way that the recipe is not the food. People sometimes confuse models of reality with reality itself.

Another crucial concept is that "Your communication is the result you get." Which means that, regardless of your intent, the important thing is what the other person understands, not what you meant to communicate. We do not see things as they are but as we are.

Talking is not the same as communicating. NLP helps us understand that communication is the sum of what we say and how we say it, including our verbal and non-verbal message. We communicate through words, voice quality and body language, through postures, gestures, and facial expressions.

Professor Mehrabian says that his studies show that 93% of the message when communicating is in the form, in how we transmit what we say, and 7% is in the words we say themselves.

Neurolinguistics also studies the power of words; depending on how you use them, you will create your thoughts, emotions, and the reality of your life. Neurolinguistics teaches us how to use our language consciously for better results in our lives. Words limit or empower us. Some examples of words that empower are "I can, I am worthy, I am capable, I am happy." Some examples of words that limit us are "I can't, but I will try, I have to," etc.

One could say that NLP scientifically proves that famous quote:

"Watch your thoughts, for they become words. Watch your words, for they become actions. Watch your actions, for they become habits. Watch your habits, for they become character. Watch your character, for it becomes your destiny."

Communication is a circle; what we do influences other people, and what they do influences us. To gain access into the other person's circle we can create *rapport* or personal attunement, which generates trust and credibility.

NLP teaches us that *rapport* or personal attunement is achieved by matching and reflecting the body language of the other person, without imitating, in a sensitive and respectful way, thus creating a bridge that improves the relationship. *Rapport* is joining each other's dance by synchronizing body language.

Relationships are born from the similarities between people. We appreciate in others the aspects that are similar to us such as style, personal tastes, values, preferences, etc.

NLP teaches us how important tone of voice (high or low), pitch (low or high), intensity and volume (audible, resonant, or submissive), and rhythm or speed of speech are in order to generate personal attunement or *rapport*. It is also necessary to consider body posture, including breathing and gestures.

Today I can understand that the important thing when communicating is not what we say but how we say it. My son did not hear my words but my despair.

I have learned that to speak from the heart what I say must be true, kind, and helpful. It is wise to speak only when what you say is better than silence.

Letters, Photos, Prayers and Poems

Álvaro Luis was an artist; his greatest desire was to achieve, through his photos and immense creativity, that people would stop to think and connect with the present, that they would observe and appreciate the beauty of places and moments, instead of taking them for granted. He loved nature, and his goal and aspiration was to create a photographic body of work with the purpose of uniting society; he wanted to shed light on a new way to understand addictions and different ways to heal them.

After sharing Álvaro's life story during a seven-day silence retreat in Joshua Tree, California, which the four of us attended as a family, the group was so moved that a fund was created to support young adults struggling and seeking peace, happiness, and a healthy life. To continue this scholarship, we created a donation box with his name. The intention is to continue helping people with life's challenges: Mindful-Way (Mindful-Way.com/Álvaro Luis Scholarship Fund).

OUR LATE SPIRITUAL SON ALVARO LUIS INSPIRED THE MINDFUL WAY PROGRAM.

After sharing the story of Alvaro's life, the group was touched and a fund was created to support young adults who are struggling and are looking for peace, happiness and healthy lives. In order to continue this scholarship we are creating a donation box in his name, with the intent of continuing to help individuals with the many joys and challenges of life.

https://www.mindful-way.com/about/Alvaro-luis-scholarship-fund/

I want to share with you the message written to us by Professor Tommy Rosen. He was the one who warmed up my soul the most after the death of my beautiful son. I also share letters and photos that I carry deep inside my heart.

I am very sorry for your loss. Álvaro's work on this plane is now over. May he rest in peace. Please remember that not everything is as it seems. Álvaro is very close to you and always will be. I am convinced that you will meet him in another way and in another place. May his family find comfort in the idea that nothing else could have been done. Álvaro's departure is part of the mystery of life.

We cannot comprehend that mystery while we are here, but we will know what the mystery is when we have to leave. Álvaro is in that place. If there is anything I can do, please let me know.

Love, strength for you and for your whole family,
Tommy Rosen

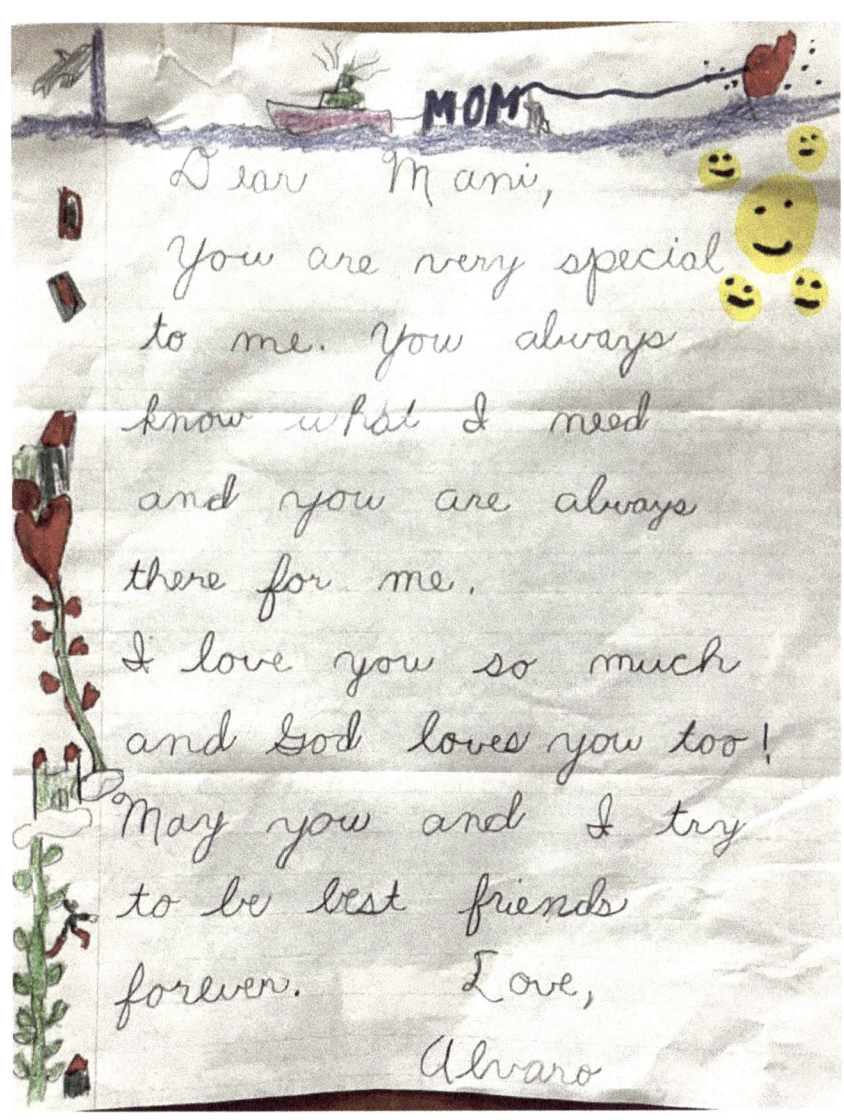

Dear Mani,

You are very special to me. You always know what I need and you are always there for me.

I love you so much and God loves you too! May you and I try to be best friends forever.

Love,

Alvaro

Praise to the Great Álvaro

I have decided to write something short and sweet, not for lack of words but because Álvaro liked things like that . . . short and sweet. Through his travels and adventures, he lived longer than anyone can dream of in many lifetimes.

I feel so grateful to have been blessed with siblings who have been not only part of my family but also my best friends and soulmates.

I spent more time with Álvaro than I have ever spent with anyone else in my entire life. And this was because I admired his every move and so I wanted to imitate his spontaneous brilliance. Every minute with him flew by. There was something in his presence that made time non-existent. The truth is that he made me feel at peace, and under his gaze, all the problems of the world dissolved. His unique and creative way of seeing life never ceased to surprise me.

I will always remember the amazing way he lit everything up without even realizing it. He was so fun and interesting that we couldn't help but make him the topic of conversation in all of our meetings.

Before we went on vacation my father always made us memorize poems and, if we didn't, he wouldn't let us go. Back then we found it unpleasant to do so. A poem entitled "If" by Rudyard Kipling reminds me a lot of Álvaro. He always repeated a line that said, "If you can meet with triumph and disaster and treat those two impostors just the same . . ."

I never really understood what this meant, but now I see that both triumph and defeat are just illusions. My brother understood this, and he did not live attached to the world of forms.

I hope one day I can learn, as he did, that what matters is not who you are as a person but who you are energetically and spiritually.

I love what Álvaro is . . . a kind and immensely loving spirit.

Santiago

Dear Brother

There are few people on this Earth with whom, when you have them in your life, a simple bond is created, regardless of where you are, who you are with, how much you have changed.

There is always an unwavering love, which unites you in any situation.

You lived your life with different rules, that were not tied to any social construct, and without prejudice. Very few people understood the world like you did.

While most people often find themselves chained to daily stressors and life plans for the future, you never let that stop you, you enjoyed the present moment.

You changed my life forever. My admiration and respect for you has always been as powerful and unfailing as the sun itself. I have never felt a spirit with as much courage as yours. And through that courage you brought me, my brother, my father and my mother, an infinite source of fortitude. Your courage and strength were so deep that you never hesitated to share it with others. Anytime we were together, all my worries would go away. It was as if the present moment was really the only thing that mattered: a song, a book, an idea.

Álvaro, in a nutshell, you changed my life forever. To lose you was to lose a best friend, a brother, and an extension of myself. Being with you for a moment dissolved all my problems instantly. The things that had once taken over my mind were now trivial and easy to do.

We had no need to argue about our concerns because your courage always motivated us. Every conversation we had, song we listened to or movie we watched, was a moment of peace and understanding. Your spirit has taught me so much so far that I am sure it will continue to travel and guide us from within.
Your brother Fernando

Dear Claudia,

Your book provides tremendous support to anyone who is trying desperately to help someone they love and is struggling to accept that their role is to love them, not to change them.

As you say, "our mission is not for our children to always lean on us, but rather for our support to eventually become unnecessary for our children." That, in and of itself, is one of the hardest things for any parent to do, and yet perhaps the most important.

What your book does is to provide immense support to anyone feeling this struggle. It does far more than just help people to visualize things differently. You provide real guidance on how to move forward. You offer "tools for finding joy after loss."

For many, who are struggling, it can feel as if you have no right to feel joy – no right to laugh. But your book provides guidance for a way back to find that joy, starting with forgiveness – forgiving oneself.

xoxo Brenda

8 MESSAGES MY SON LEFT TO RECOVER JOY

Forgiveness

The only way to understand and process everything is by forgiving. Your presence is infinite; your spirit is my spirit; your peace is my peace.

Grounding

Your walk on this earth connects and transforms the hearts of those who are open and receptive. Your presence is infinite, only your form changes. Thank you for existing.

Mindfulness

Living in the present moment increases our health and well-being. Being stuck in the past or the future prevents us from flowing in harmony. Being present is the way.

Breathing

Focus your attention on your inhalation and exhalation, observe your thoughts, and let them go. Repeat, and you are meditating.

Morning Habits

Your powerful, loving spirit inspires the whole world to have compassion. You planted peace in our hearts and taught us to accept things as they are. Thank you for your light!

Gratitude

Nothing happens by accident. We are where we need to be right now. We must trust and focus only on becoming the best versions of ourselves.

Visualization

Your dreams are magic. Build them into your life with passion.

Purpose and Meaning

I ask the Universe to put me in the places it wants me to be, with the people it wants me to be with.

There Is No Death

John Lucky McCreery

There is no death! The stars go down'
To rise upon some other shore,
And bright in heaven's jeweled crown
They shine for evermore.

There is no death! The dust we tread
Shall change, beneath the summer showers,
To golden grain, or mellow fruit,
Or rainbow-tinged flowers.
[...]
And ever near us, though unseen,
The dear immortal spirits tread;
For all the boundless universe
Is life—there are no dead.

Where There Is Love

Robert Holden

Where there is love,
pain breathes,
tears smile,
hurt softens,
guilt loses its edge,
judgment forgets to judge,
fear is no longer afraid,
separation is over:
Where there is love,
You are there.

Poem by Mother Teresa

People are often unreasonable, illogical, and self-centered:
Forgive them anyway.
If you are kind, people may accuse you self-ish ulterior motives:
Be kind anyway.
If you are successful, you will win some false friends and true enemies:
Succeed anyway.
If you are honest and frank people will try to cheat you:
Be honest anyway.
What you spend years building, someone can destroy overnight:
Build anyway.
If you find serenity and happiness, they may be jealous of you:
Be happy anyway.
The good you do today, will often be forgot-ten by tomorrow:
Do good anyway.

Give the world the best you have, and it may never be enough:

Give your best anyway.

You see, in the final analysis, it is between you and God.

It was never between you and them anyway.

Prayer of St. Francis of Assisi

Lord, make me an instrument of your peace.
Where there is hatred, let me sow love;
where there is injury, pardon;
where there is doubt, faith;
where there is despair, hope;
where there is darkness, light;
and where there is sadness, joy.
O Divine Master, grant that I may not so much seek
to be consoled as to console;
to be understood as to understand;
to be loved as to love.
For it is in giving that we receive,
it is in pardoning that we are pardoned,
and it is in dying that we are born to eternal life.
Amen.

Álvaro Luis, you are a loving and brilliant spirit, thank you for brightening our life!
We will love you forever.

ACKNOWLEDGMENTS

I thank my wonderful life partner for believing in me and loving me unconditionally.

To my children, Santiago and Fernando, I thank you for your sweetness and compassion; it is a great honor and privilege to be your mother. I admire and am very proud of you. You are examples of brave and enterprising human beings, committed to your mission of bringing light, health, and life to humanity.

I thank all my extended family and friends for their support and help in turning the conflict of the disease of addiction into growth. Thank you, I love you.

I thank my sister Márgara for showing me how to be resilient, and to Jerry my talented nephew for his kind proofreading of this book.

I thank my sisters-in-law for their generous hearts.

Thanks to my favorite and amazing belly dance teacher, Portia Lange, who supported me producing the eight exercises video together with lovely Fernanda and Marite.

I thank and remember with great affection all the teachers who loved Álvaro Luis and recognized his talent, brilliance, and kind soul. I wish I remembered each of their names, but right now what I remember most is their loving presence in my son's life. I especially thank:

The art teacher at Gulliver who told me, "Your son has extraordinary artistic talent."

The Spanish teacher Inés Pearson of Miami Country Day school who invited him to all her special events.

The adorable Sister Rosie, a second-grade teacher at Epiphany (and all the Epiphany community) who taught me that even if only one letter of Álvaro's handwriting homework was well done, we should focus our attention on that and congratulate him.

The South African piano teacher who chose my son's photo for the cover of the show and always gave him extra time and candy.

His amazing tennis teacher, Daniel Spatz, who enjoyed my son's brilliant conversation (his friend

Gabriel would ask him, "How can you talk so smart?").

I thank doctor and author Paula Petry for her unconditional support and her example of love and professionalism.

To Beth Mulligan and Hugh O'Neil for their compassionate connection to our family and their help in creating the Scholarship Fund for young people in mindfulness retreats.

Thanks to Professor Lawrence Huff for inviting me to work in prisons; it has been the space where my son's spirit has manifested itself the most and I have been able to expand my heart.

To Mr. Barber, director of the Miami Rescue Mission center, for his advice and hospitality toward my family.

To Pablo Landi, Landmark's extraordinary leader, for his connection, compassion, and support for my family.

To Rafael Pérez, Kundalini yoga teacher, acupuncturist, and exceptional healer.

To Vic Muñoz, my first yoga teacher, who worked with my son Álvaro Luis and always sought to help him.

To Dr. Canali for his big heart.

To my Mindfulness teacher, Fleet Maull.

To my coaching teacher, Arturo Orantes.

I thank my professor Tommy Rosen for his absolute dedication to awakening humanity and redefining success.

To Dr. Juan Carlos Paredes, known as Dr. Joy, founder of South Beach Clinic at Mount Sinai Hospital in Miami Beach, thank you for believing in me and hiring me to collaborate with your patients. I wholeheartedly admire the integrative and functional psychiatry you practice.

To Dr. San Pal for her questions to guide my personal growth.

To all my unconditional friends, thank you for your great support and affection.

To all the support groups, for providing the space where I have been able to grow and feel the loving connection of the Universe.

To my friend Rosita (ROO) Escalante for being an exemplary warrior. I thank life for witnessing your tenacity; you are an inspiration. You have managed to paint a divine and prolific collection of wonderful art with your mouth. Your work as a motivator is extraordinary. Thank you for listening and supporting me. You are a wonderful being.

To Juan Pablo Ospina and Gerardo Alzugaray, immense thanks for your patience and support in the huge technological challenge that completing this book has been for me.

I am very grateful for the loving and generous collaboration of Bri Martinez for her great talent in the animation of the drawings. The plan is perfect, and you are a treasure!

To my editor and translator Gloria Noriega, thank you for being part of this project, you are extraordinary.

Thank you Amalia Restrepo for your beautiful cover illustrations.

To everyone I forgot to mention, know that you have been a great inspiration and support for this book. Thank you!

"I am immensely grateful to God for taking me by the hand and leading me to heal my heart."

Harvest joy now

Thank you for embracing this book and allowing it into your hands. Consider gifting yourself a transformative coaching session with me at chateodelcorazon.com/services

Bibliography and Recommended Reading

Beattie, Melody, *The New Codependency*, Simon & Schuster Paperbacks, 2009.

Chödrön, Pema, *The Wisdom of No Escape*, Shambhala Publications, Boston, 2001.

Clark, Carol, *Addict America: The Lost Connection*, Carol L. Clark, 2011.

De Pape, Baptist, The Power of the Heart: Find Your True Purpose in Life, Simon & Schuster, Inc., 2014.

Elrod, Hal, David, Anna, Polish, Joe, *et al.*, *The Miracle Morning for Addiction Recovery*, Hal Elrod International Inc., 2018.

Field, Tiffany, *Touch*, Bradford Books, 2014.

Hay, Louise, *You Can Heal Your Life*, Hay House, Inc., 2004.

Hendrix, Harville, LaKelly Hunt, Helen, *The Space Between: The Point of Connection*, Clovercroft Publishing, 2017.

Holden, Robert, *Finding Love Everywhere*, Hay House, Inc., 2020.

Hudson, John, Meditation: Simple Steps to Peace, Well-Being, and Contentment: How to Quieten Your Mind and Enhance Your Health and Life Through the Art of Stillness, Southwater, 2007.

Khouri, Hala, *Peace From Anxiety*, Shambhala Publications, Inc., 2021.

Kornfield, Jack, *No Time Like the Present*, Atria Books, 2017.

Lozoff, Bo, We're All Doing Time: A Guide for Getting Free, Human Kindness Foundation, 2017.

Neufeld, Gordon and Mate, Gabor, Hold on to Your Kids: Why Parents Need to Matter More *Than Peers*, Ballantine Books, N.Y., 2014.

Niemiec, Ryan M., McGrath, Robert E., The Power of Character Strengths: Appreciate and *Ignite Your Positive Personality*, VIA Institute on Character, 2019.

Rohr, Richard, *Everything Belongs: The Gift of Contemplative Prayer*, Crossroads Publishing Company, N.Y., 2003.

Rosen, Tommy, Recovery 2.0: Move Beyond Addiction and Upgrade Your Life, Hay House, Inc., 2014.

Ross, Julia, The Mood Cure: The 4-Step Program to Take Charge of Your Emotion— *Today*, Penguin Books, 2002.

Sampson, Chere M., *Can You See What Eye See?*, Balboa Press, 2019.

Seaward, Brian Luke, Managing Stress: Principles and Strategies for Health and *Well-Being*, Jones & Bartlett Publishers, 2014, Fourth Edition.

Thich, Nhat Hanh, True Love: A Practice for Awakening the Heart, Shambhala Publications, Boulder Colorado, 2004.

Tsabary, Shefali, The Awakened Family: A Revolution in Parenting, Viking, 2016.

Walton, David, A Practical Guide to Emotional Intelligence: Get Smart About Emotion (Practical Guide Series), MJF Books, 2012.

Westmacott-Brown, Nathalia, *Breathwork: A Little Book of Self Care*, Penguin Random House, 2019.

Access for free our exclusive video to heal your heart.

Discover 8 simple exercises that I practice daily with my loved ones, empowering me to open and connect with my spine. I sincerely hope they contribute to your journey as well.

Join our mindful community and participate in future events!

chateodelcorazon.com/giftvideo

IMPORTANT REQUEST!

Thank you immensely for journeying through
the pages of our book!

Your engagement and feedback mean the world to me,
and I deeply value your insights.

To enhance both this book and those to come,
your input is invaluable.

Could I kindly ask for just a moment of your time to share your
thoughts with a review on Amazon? Your review will shape the
future versions of this book and my upcoming works.

With heartfelt gratitude,
Claudia C. Castillo